UNDERSTANDING MODERN ART

UNDERSTANDING
MODERN ART

❊❊❊❊❊❊❊

BY
MORRIS DAVIDSON

1934
TUDOR PUBLISHING CO.
NEW YORK

TO

A · S · D

FOREWORD

·➤➤·➤➤·◄◄·◄◄·

It is my conviction that no one can really understand modern painting who has not first understood the motivating spirit of all Western painting. For this reason so much space has been given to a discussion of the traditional forms. Instead of just rapture I have tried to show the evolutionary process of European painting which culminated in the puzzling pictures we see about us to-day. The puzzle then solves itself. M. D.

CONTENTS

-»»-»»-«-««-

PART THREE: *The Evolution of Modern Art*

LIST OF ILLUSTRATIONS

❧❧❧❧

PART ONE

An Appreciation of Painting

1

SOME CONSIDERATIONS
OF PAINTING

➤➤ ➤➤ ◄◄ ◄◄

THE INTEREST in matters of art has never been so widespread in this country as at present. It may be that the pioneering need for keeping our noses to the grindstone is gradually passing away, and although few of us are individuals of abundant leisure, most of us can find time to devote to pursuits other than the purely economic and the purely social. We have discovered play. But we have found, too, that mere diversion is not satisfying; we look for some interest which touches us more deeply than play.

17

Sometimes it is a mystical cult, more often it is art. Art itself is mystical—a riddle which fascinates, but challenges our understanding. How can we fathom its secrets?

In metropolitan cities there is no dearth of exhibitions of contemporary art, and of the art of the past. Whether we are in easy access of them or not we make our pilgrimage to these shrines of art. We tread the soft carpets lightly; a feeling akin to religious emotion makes us move about in awe. Our catalogue in hand, we match the number in the little disk at the side of each picture and then search for information about the genius who painted it. What do we find? The name of the picture, the name of the artist, and the name of the millionaire who so kindly loaned the picture to the gallery. We are thrown upon our emotional reactions. We walk about bewildered, faintly attracted to some canvases more than to others, without knowing why, without any feeling except that we are standing in the presence of something which mankind regards as much more than an ornament to life. We have something of the mystical, the religious feeling, but we prefer a more positive appreciation which can come only through understanding. So we go to the critics and philosophers.

That is, we read or try to read their books. We spend hours in bookshops looking over volumes that claim to hold the secret of what is art, and what is beauty, and what is good and bad painting. We look carefully to see how many pictures are reproduced, and whether the type is easy to read. When we finally select the book that promises most,

1. THE CHAIR—VAN GOGH

**2. THE AWAKENING OF SPRING—
EMIL FUCHS**

*Reproduced by permission of G. P. Putnam's Sons, publishers of "With
Pencil, Brush and Chisel," by Emil Fuchs, and The Guaranty Trust
Company of New York, Executors of the Fuchs Estate.*

we take it under our arm already satisfied that next week we shall be able to exposé to others the values and meaning of pictures. There is a glow in our hearts when we remove our shoes and relax in our easy chairs ready to begin reading. We turn the fly leaf, read the dedication to "my wife Mary," wonder what she's like, and plunge into the first paragraph. But in half an hour we have been assailed by so many unfamiliar terms that require special definitions, not even to be found in the dictionary, that we abandon the reading and look at the pictures.

Our disappointment is due not to the books so much as to the nature of art criticism itself. It has invented its own language. We have not as yet been trained in this strange tongue because writers have not taken the trouble to teach us its vocabulary. If we are led gradually along to an understanding of terms we may return to these books and find them surprisingly fruitful, even exciting.

Often the illustrations which we thumb through in books whose purpose it is to enlighten us, displease us and make us defiant. Rationalize as we will, we are convinced that we shall never care for the picture. This is an attitude we must suspend if we are to find pleasure in pictures. Taste is a precarious scale for weighing art, unless it is an educated taste. The waspish Whistler was once greatly annoyed by a nice old lady who insisted on pointing out to him the good and bad pictures in an exhibition. The great painter objected to her positive judgments. "Well," said the old lady, "I may not know anything about art, but I certainly

19

know what I like." "A prerogative, madam, shared by the lower animals," replied the artist.

The questions arise: "What is an educated taste? Who can rightfully lay claim to it? If the artist possesses it, how is it that Cezanne saw nothing good in the work of his illustrious contemporaries or that artists have always been notoriously prone to hold each other's work in small esteem? Are there really any standards in painting? Are not all intelligent, sensitive persons, in spite of Whistler's sarcasm, entitled to their own free opinions regarding art?

The last question is the easiest. The answer is yes. The man who cherishes magazine covers, frames them, hangs them in his den would be brutally deprived of a factor in the pleasure of living were his "art" confiscated by a Society for the Suppression of Bad Pictures. If "bad art" gives us pleasure let no critic rob us of that rare commodity. Upon this point we readily reach agreement. The difficulty begins when the man who owns the picture insists that it is *good* art.

"No one appreciates a sunset more than I do," he will protest. "I have stood for hours watching the fading of one glorious color into another. I feel as qualified to pass on matters of beauty as any artist. Beautiful forms stop the beating of my heart. The melodies of Mozart send me into ecstasy. And I am not merely emotional. I am a discriminating, critical, logical person, certainly not intellectually inferior to an artist. The artist prates of that mystifying thing 'the esthetic experience.' He feels superior

20

to people like me because he feels he has had it, and we have not. I submit that Mozart, the sunsets, the shadowy forms of night are as much esthetic experience as any that he has had."

The fallacy of this argument is that there are the common experiences or reactions to beautiful sights, sounds, smells, etc. which great numbers of mortals may enjoy, and there are the special experiences which are had only within the realm, not of Art, but of *each* art. The man who has coddled a musical instrument until the sound of two particular notes throws him into ecstasy, will look coldly, if at all, at two juxtaposed colors which affect the painter just as strongly. The painter in turn may pass the world's masterpieces of sculpture without lifting an eyebrow. The sculptor may be deaf to the intricacies and joys of the musician's counterpoint. All three may scorn the theater. An "artistic" nature, then, is not a passport through the realms of all the arts.

Positive judgment or taste is too often the result of some personal limitation. We may have myopia or infantile fixations. If we are vegetarians we recoil in horror at the sight of a gory picture by Delacroix. To say that Delacroix was therefore a bad painter would be unfair. Some of us, neither vegetarians nor socialists, prefer certain colors to others. The psychologists call these decided preferences fetishes. Whatever they are they influence, unjustly, our opinions of pictures.

Last, but by no means least important is self-hypnosis

21

which passes for an educated taste. Our awe for famous names leads us often to imagine that we are desperate devotees of painters whose pictures we do not understand at all. This is true particularly of certain wealthy collectors. If they buy for investment or ultimate profit that is a different matter. But many of them buy famous names because of the feeling that sole possession of the canvas in some patent way gives them the exclusive right to an understanding of it. Their love for paintings proves to be mere snobbery.

A false appreciation of painting is no greater obstacle to an understanding than the obstinacy which comes from the wish to be let alone. Most people are comfortable as they are and do not wish to be disturbed with new ideas. Together with those who mourn a bygone era they have taken as their proverb the saying: "There is nothing new under the sun."

The artist seems designed by nature to combat the superstition that there is nothing new under the sun. However unwelcome he may be to them, he keeps plain citizens from fossilizing in spite of themselves. His business is, secondarily, to show that there are always new things under the sun if you only know how to look for them. We say secondarily because the primary purpose of the artist is to enjoy himself at his work; or stated another way, the artist paints because he is unhappy if he doesn't.

When we say that the business of the artist is to show people new things to look at, we do not mean that it is necessary for him to explore the ice fields of the polar regions in order to find a new type of icicle to hold up to our attention. He will look at the familiar object which has met our gaze for years, and whereas we see it always in the same commonplace way, just a chair, or a broken pitcher, he will show us how beautiful the thing can be if looked at for its color, its design, and for other qualities which we shall explain later. If he is a genius he will show us how beautiful the thing is by painting it as if it never before existed, yet without destroying its identity. He gets the golden egg without killing the goose.

Van Gogh accomplished this feat. He saw new beauty in the most ordinary objects. While he achieved his effects largely through the use of color, his odd, original way of seeing things is apparent even in the black and white reproduction of his *Chair* (Fig. 1). Before Van Gogh no painter thought a chair sufficiently interesting to want to paint a portrait of it. Nor did any painter think of painting a single object looking down upon it from above. The thing has been done since many thousands of times. But it required a genius to see enough beauty in an old, familiar object to want to paint its portrait, and show us a new aspect of it.

Yet nothing is more difficult, at first, than the task of showing us something new. The story of painting is full of incidents illustrating how shocking it has been to various publics to have some new view of an old thing put before it. The English painter Constable, who is generally considered the father of modern landscape painting, met with the

greatest opposition from the official artists to whom painting was a highly respectable and orthodox craft, like sad-
dlemaking. His boldness in daring to mix a little green
color with brown when he painted the grass in his pictures
struck consternation in the hearts of the conservative
Academicians. In all the paintings since the beginning of
British art grass was recorded with brown paint. Therefore
it was brown. Constable was either color-blind or an heretic.
To save himself from being burned as a witch, or at least
from being kept out of the Royal Academy, he led a committee of professors out to the nearest meadows, got down
on his knees, and with a blob of paint at the end of a stick
showed them then and there that the grass was identical
with the green on the stick. The committee wagged their
heads in amazement. But from that time on grass was
green, except to staid dullards and die-hards.

All of us are familiar with the famous libel suit brought
by Whistler against Ruskin. The cultured Ruskin had seen
and studied everything of importance in the world of art.
He was the greatest critic of his time. If quantity is impressive, he was the most voluminous art critic of all time.
You had only to show him an oddly shaped doughnut to
set him off on another volume. Yet this cultured, indulgent
man became abusive at the sight of a sketch by Whistler
because it was something entirely new to him. "The im-
pudence of this coxcomb in asking a hundred guineas for
flinging a pot of paint in the face of the public!" he wrote.
The court awarded the artist a farthing damages. But

24

Whistler's greater vindication has come from thousands of people throughout the world.

Now if we agree that an artist is a person who is able to show us new aspects of familiar things, it follows that one who shows us the same old stuff over and over again is not an artist. He is merely a craftsman, or as some will have it, a potboiler. He takes advantage of the wish of people not to be disturbed by anything new, and provides them with the kind of art *which was once art,* but which is now only an imitation of art, or merchandise. A picture which does not present some new and vital aspect of a familiar object or subject can add nothing to our pleasure except as decoration (something to cover the wall), or as a possession (something to make the neighbors envious).

We have cleared away much brush. We have considered the usual obstacles in the way of an appreciation of painting. Feelings of special competence and the wish to be let alone, to repeat a bygone tradition, are the most common. If we can avoid these states we are ready for something constructive. There are general laws or precepts in painting as there are in physics.

For instance, a work of art must not stimulate in the beholder loathing or desire. A cartoon that makes us boil to kill the brutal soldiers who are shown running their bayonets through little babes is not art—it is illustration. The poster that prompts us to part with our cash for a car which we have no use for, or an investment bond, is illustration. Any pictorial representation which takes our

25

minds away from *itself* is illustration. Any picture which advertises a product, or sentiment, whether it is done in oil or in pen and ink or in electric lights, is illustration.

Some illustration *can* be art. When the picture is done with such skill and talent and with such adherence to the qualities of painting that the picture itself holds our interest more than the story it tells, then it is art. The old masterpieces of the Renaissance, which we go to see in the museums, tell the story of the Bible. But so definitely do they possess the qualities of painting, that, while illustration, their claim to art is unquestioned. In looking at them we lose sight of their advertising value for Christianity. They are poor advertising but good art. We shall see later that many of the painters of these pictures and their patrons were really not Christians but pagans.

Often it is the way the painter looks at his subject that determines whether his picture is or is not art. This is easy to explain. On page 27 is a line known as Hogarth's *Line of Beauty*. It is nice to look at. When you sign your name with a flourish you make a curve something like it. The English artist Hogarth discovered this line for himself while looking at the profile of a nude woman's back. When he looked at the nude back he detached it in his mind from any thoughts or feelings about women. At the moment his enjoyment was complete in looking at the line. The line possessed *esthetic* value for him.

But if we think of this line not as a decorative thing in itself but as the back of a nude woman who is winking her

26

3. BATHER ARRANGING HER HAIR—RENOIR

4. THE GOLDEN WEDDING ANNIVERSARY—
COLMAIRE

eye, it ceases to have esthetic value for us. It suggests other
things. It becomes illustration, like the poster and the cartoon. And whether or not we fall to daydreaming about
nudes, the art in the line does not exist any more for us.
It is destroyed.

The nude has many other beautiful lines. It has as many

beautiful forms, considering them by themselves, or related to each other. They are beautiful when you think only
of their appearance and not of their meaning, function,
etc., when you think of them *abstractly*. Abstractly means
literally, drawn away from. When we draw these forms and
lines away from any association with the purpose or function or desirability of woman and look at them for the
beauty that is in them, or abstractly, we are looking at the
art in the nude. But if we enjoy studying the photographs
in the so-called "Art" magazines it shows that we are not

27

so much concerned with art as we are with other projects, perhaps divorce.

Since so much depends upon which way we react to a nude, it would seem impossible to say which nude is art and which plain pornography. But this query may be solved. We have only to ask ourselves: Did the artist paint his model with the purpose of arousing our emotions? Or did he paint the abstract beauties before him? By this means we shall find how simple it is to sift the nudes which are painted from the point of view of art, from those whose purpose it seems is to advertise Miss Ruby De La Rue, artist's model.

An advertising drawing or an illustration is not elevated to a higher place as art merely because it is done in the same *technique* as the finest masterpieces. Technique means only the brushwork, the mechanics. If you are sawing a piece of wood, holding the saw with both hands, your technique is funny. Some people run in the style of a galloping elephant. Their technique is bad. They prefer to use an elephant's technique, just as many excellent illustrators prefer to use the technique of the painter, instead of drawing with pen and ink.

We shall see further on in the book that most of the opposition towards Modernist painters has arisen because of the confusion between illustration and painting. In Anglo-Saxon countries it is still rare for a painter to be taken seriously who paints *things* instead of *stories about things*. The Mother and Babe theme, the Hunt, the Rescue, etc.,

28

are fastened in the minds of the citizenry as standards for all generations of artists. Fortunately the influence of the French has begun to be felt, even in Anglo-Saxon countries.

The French attitude is one of objectivity. Let us see for instance what was in the mind of Van Gogh (a Dutchman, it is true, but French in his painting attitude) when he painted his chair. He did not wish to sell us the chair. This is plain because it is presented to us truthfully, as he saw it, without any desire to gloss over its defects, or to make the paint appear like polished Duco. He looked at the chair objectively, as a scientist looks at an ant. The scientist wishes to learn something and to tell us something about the ant; he does not wish to sell it to us, or to make it appear beautiful so that we become eager to have one in our home. Van Gogh was just as objective.

Now if he had placed a tack on the chair, the picture would not be objective. It would become an illustration. We should be compelled in spite of any nice intentions to think of the expression on the face of the person who might sit down on the tack. This idea would so overshadow the good painting in the picture that the whole thing would cease to be art, and would become a cartoon in the technique of an oil painting.

When the artist paints his *feelings* on looking at the object, when he wants to give us his editorial comment, or show his reactions to the thing he is painting, he becomes *subjective*. We shall return to this term later.

Before we begin the story of painting, however, we must,

29

as we said before, understand the meanings of terms, the vocabulary of painting. Terms are necessary not only to criticize pictures but to explain what the painter has in mind, if only subconsciously, when he works. The notion that he has nothing in mind except to copy literally what he sees is common but fallacious. The painter does not literally copy what is before him.

The story has been told in many schoolrooms of how the ancient Greeks held a contest to select the greatest painter from among them. The painter Zeuxis who had distinguished himself by his pictures of mythological scenes entered the competition. Instead of painting men and women, he wished to demonstrate his superiority in a way that would be conclusive. He painted a bunch of grapes, perhaps the first still-life in the history of art. So real did the grapes appear that birds flew towards the canvas and pecked at it. Needless to say, the legend has him acclaimed the greatest painter of Athens.

It is obvious that the person who invented this anecdote regarded the accurate copy of nature the end of art. But it is also obvious that he was not alive in the time of Praxiteles and Phidias. Greece has been called the home of Classical art, because its artists and sculptors were *not* content to copy what was before them, but sought a system of proportion, an ideal or model for perfection in the human form. Its system has been handed down to us through the centuries and we retain the Greek ideal of proportion in

30

the human figure. The name Classical has always meant, as it does today, the reverse of Realistic.

Not only is it impossible for a mature artist to copy literally from nature—because his training, taste, experiences, have all "set"—but the aim is furthest from his intentions. He leaves copying to those who have nothing important to tell us of their own discoveries in nature. If a person has no new aspect to show us he is a painter, but not an artist. Every quality the artist incorporates in his picture will bear the stamp of his personality. He cannot be literal, as a child is, without being consciously so. What happens is that he develops a color sense which makes it necessary for him to change the colors before him in nature to conform to his taste. He does the same with all the other attributes or special qualities of painting.

We shall first find out what these qualities are. Once we can identify them when we see them, it will matter little whether we prefer one painter to another. Our preferences are important only to psychologists. But instead of limiting our pleasure in pictures to what we like, we may find a limitless pleasure in looking at pictures for the good that is in them. We cannot arrive at a universal accord in taste, but we can come to a fairly clear understanding of what the painter set out to do. In this way we can find pleasure without demanding (what is our notion of) perfection.

2

PAINTING QUALITIES
AND TRAITS

❯❯❯ ❯❯❯ ❮❮❮ ❮❮❮

THE PURPOSE of the music composer is to discover new and original combinations of notes. To most people *newness* is a disturbance, as we have already seen. But for the composer to lay any serious claim to the title of artist, the first, most fundamental requisite is that he invent something new with notes.

He may create new melodies, or invent new harmony, or make innovations in counterpoint. These are only a few of the qualities of music which he can attain by means of

32

notes. Melody alone is not enough to give his composition
any great value as art.

Now if music is the art of notes, painting is the art—
not of color, as some critics will have it, but—of paint.
Color is only one of the qualities in painting, as melody
is only one of the qualities of music. The painter uses paint
to attain *color harmony, form, design,* and other attributes.
Color is no more the complete attainment for the painter
than is the tune for the music composer.

Color requires explanation. We said in the last chapter
that every painter in the course of his experience with
colors works out a scheme or relationship which best
expresses his personality. Often there is some psychological reason for a painter's preference for certain colors.
For example a tender poetic nature may be reflected in
deep warm tones. Since a painter's color is a personal
matter, it is more properly *his trait* and not a quality of
painting.

Design embodies color, but it serves a different purpose.
So we shall give it special consideration. Design is the
general head under which is grouped *pattern* and *rhythm.*
Sometimes it is called *organization,* sometimes *composition.* It means only the arrangement of the space in a
canvas so that the message or statement of the artist is conveyed to us with clarity, with unity, with forcefulness, and
with grace. The artist is confronted by a rectangle of canvas. He must put down what he has to say in an effective
way and in an appealing way. There are two prominent

33

means by which he can do it, those mentioned above under the general head of design.

Pattern is the most common means of achieving clarity and grace. The artist who chooses to compose his picture by means of pattern simply divides his canvas into a colored map. If we look at a map we see that each state is a different color, and a different shape, and a different size. Pattern in a picture is exactly the same thing. It possesses only one additional feature: If we could make a map without using color and still make each state distinct, how should we do it? We could do it by different kinds of dots or crosses or other marks, but the easiest way would be to make each state a different shade of dark or light. In painting, each shade is called a *value*. The painter, in addition to striving for a variety of colors, strives for a variety of values. The prime essential, the *sine qua non* of pattern is variety. Without variety the pattern is not valid as art because it cannot hold our interest and attention. The good painter must be a good psychologist. At least he must know that variety is the spice of life.

On the opposite page are two sketches. The first one is monotonous in its pattern, there is no variety in its shapes and values. It has only two values, white and dark. The second sketch does possess variety; there are three values, and the shapes and sizes of each area, or pattern, are different.

Pattern can be abstract, that is, it can be beautiful in itself without meaning anything. A piece of cretonne or a

34

5. THE TWO CLOWNS—DAUMIER

6. MOONLIGHT ON THE LAKE —
DIDIER-POUGET

rug possesses pattern which is only decorative or ornamental and means nothing. In painting, however, the artist
usually tries to fit his objects into a pattern so that the picture is not only beautiful but represents something besides.

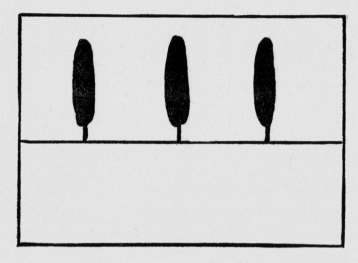

An outline of a horse may make a beautiful pattern, just as the drawing of a monkey's tail may make a beautiful line.

This brings us to some consideration of *line*. The scribble of a pencil, the carefully made contour of an ornate church steeple are both line. A line may express something or it may be purely decorative. When it expresses something it is called *functional*, because it does some work, performs some function. A functional line can be compared to a housemaid; a decorative line, to a beautiful and idle girl. "Beauty is its own excuse," says the poet.

How can we know which line is beautiful and which not? Let us trust our taste in this one instance because our preference is instinctive. Art is an artifice of man and our instincts help us little to understand it. But line is an element of nature borrowed by the artist from nature. The gnarled and knotty tree does not attract us as does the graceful, elegant tree. The bulbous nose does not attract us as does the straight one. Regularity, a certain geometrical system of proportion, variable to be sure, guides us in our tastes. We may have preferences for short squat women or tall thin ones, but when we look for beauty disinterestedly, we prefer regularly proportioned women with regularly formed features as instinctively as we prefer a regular handwriting to a scrawl. The commercial theater is built upon this premise. The baby is horrified by the kind-hearted friend of the family whose face is so grotesque. Ichabod Crane could not command the respect of

36

his scholars because they could not accept nor admire his peculiar or irregular proportions. So that we see that preference is instinctive and we are to have no qualms about beautiful line.

But line can be decorative even when it is not beautiful. When it is used in repetition throughout a canvas it can be unpleasant in itself and still create a pleasant effect. This

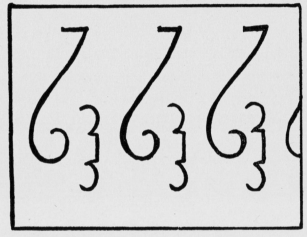

effect is as valid, as a design, as is pattern, and is preferred by many artists. Let us look at the above sketch. Two lines are used as a basis for the design. When these lines are repeated we call them motifs. The upper motif is pleasant or decorative in itself; the lower motif is not. Together the two produce a kind of design which is called *rhythm*.

Why, we may ask, does a motif, which is in itself unattractive, please us so when it is repeated, when it is rhythmic? Possibly because it suggests movement. Our

37

eye is taken from the thing itself to the repetition. When we walk or run or hop, we repeat the same motion. We repeat it with regularity. And if there are more motions than one repeated, we are all the more fascinated. For instance, it is more interesting to watch an athlete hop, step, and jump than to watch him run in a marathon race. Music thrills us because the different cadences and rhythms are repeated. Dancing is the rhythmic repetition of a few motions. The rhythmic beat of the drum can excite us, as well as any savages, to such a pitch that we want to fight. Activity, motion, movement are suggested by rhythm. The porpoise does not interest us enough to draw us to the aquarium. But we will spend hours on a steamer deck waiting to see it leap out of the water. We are not fascinated because it leaps out of the water, but because it leaps out of the water rhythmically.

Like pattern, rhythm can be abstract, that is, it can exist merely as a decoration; or the artist can fit his objects, figures, lights and shadows into the lines, so that they are made to express the movement of the motif, or motifs. The painter may use rhythm to convey to us emotional states of mind, excitement and ecstasy.

Now let us return to functional line which we left dangling in mid-air. When the painter uses line to create the illusion of reality, he must use functional line. On the opposite page is a line which can make no claim to beauty or even interest by itself. It is not decorative. But when we see it as the nose of some one it immediately takes on significance. It tells us something. It is not only the portrait of some one's nose, it suggests the entire person.

When in addition to suggesting or representing, it creates the illusion of roundness or form or bulk of an object, it becomes an important quality of painting. For instance,

when the artist wishes to give us the illusion of a saucepan he can do it by functional line. If he drew it like the sketch below it would fail to convince us; but by giving us the illusion of the space inside of the thing, as in the object

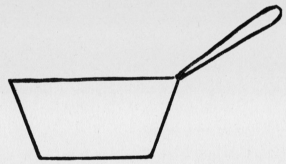

shown on page 40, he does convince us of its form by the functional line of the ellipse.

It is seldom, however, that the good painter depends upon functional line to obtain the illusion of form. Form to a painter is often the most serious problem of all, the

39

most sought-after quality of painting. He tries to achieve it not so much by line as by color and by values. Color we know means the manner in which *colors* are used by each artist.

Values, we have seen, means the degree of light and shade in a picture. (Italians call it *chiaroscuro*, as do art critics.) If the lights in a painting are very light, and the darks very dark, we say the values are strong, if we like

the picture; and too harsh, or too sharp, if we don't like it. If, on the other hand, a picture appears smoky and woolly and confused, we say the painter has no sense of values. His values are weak. Again if his lights jump out of the canvas instead of lying quiet, and his darks look like accidental smudges due to careless handling on the part of the expressman, we say the values are false.

We shall see presently how values are used in obtaining form. But let us first determine whether we know what form is. It is the opposite of flatness. It is not present in a sheet of paper, for instance. A sheet of paper has no form,

40

it has only area. But if we crumple it in any way so that it is no longer completely flat, it takes on form. A circle is flat, it has no form; it has only area, which differs from the area in the sheet of paper only in its geometric shape. A sphere, on the other hand, has form. Anything that has depth, or thickness, or volume, has form. If we feel that we can run our hands *around* an object instead of just over it, we know it has form.

The artist who is really devoted to form is an entirely different genus from the artist who cares only about the surface aspect of things. In looking at an object the former is aware that there are other qualities present in it. Color, values, texture, etc. But like a true lover and monogamist, he has eyes only for form. He makes the others slaves who do her bidding. The result is apparent to the spectator. The spectator is made to feel that he is touching the painted object with his eyes, if not with his fingers.

The artist employs a system for controlling the light in his picture of an object. He does not paint the lights and shadows as he sees them at first glance, or as the camera would record them. He manipulates his values. For instance, in painting a ball, he sternly harnesses the light, confining it to the one place that will best reveal the form, as in the sketch shown on page 42. Even if the ball were made of glass which would catch numerous lights and reflections, the artist intent upon form would minimize their importance.

The strips which give the appearance of latitude and

longitude lines to the ball are of course merely a device to indicate how the painter separates the values. Each little part or segment is called a *plane*. There are planes of light and planes of dark. Cezanne painted with planes of color. The purpose of planes is to create the illusion of reality

more intensely than nature itself. A photograph is so subtle in its values that the best it can do is to *suggest* reality. It cannot give us an intensified illusion of reality. A plane puts into one little space the simplified and condensed expression of that space. It is a more emphatic way of saying something. The difference between the painter's way of stating a fact and the camera's is similar to the difference in speech when we say, leaning out of the window,

42

7. SAINTE VICTOIRE MOUNTAIN—CEZANNE

8. HOMAGE TO DELACROIX — FANTIN-LATOUR
Courtesy Giraudon, Paris

"Officer, I am having difficulty extinguishing a blaze which started in the kitchen. Won't you turn in an alarm, please?" as opposed to the dramatic cry, "Fire!"

The first statement is a cool collection of facts without emotional urge. There is no indication of stress or distress, and while such calm speech is Spartan and greatly admired in some circles, it nevertheless fails to convey the urgency of the situation and is inhuman in its mechanical method. The cry "Fire!" on the other hand, is the only important word necessary. It stresses the urgency of the situation and conveys it to everybody. It omits the unnecessary words "kitchen," "difficulty," "alarm." It is concerned with only one thing, fire. So when we say the camera is like the first statement we mean that it gives equal mechanical importance to a mass of unimportant detail while the artist expends himself on one urgent, condensed statement, and does it often by means of planes.

Some teachers of art, in stressing the importance of exercising selection in painting from nature, say, "Nature is not good enough. It is the business of the artist to improve upon it." It is usually the potboilers and the sentimentalists who feel the necessity for improving the appearance of nature. The mother who wishes to improve the appearance of her tough little Willie has exactly the same snobbish urge. Real artists who paint nature do not actually want to improve nature, they want to present it to us, *in one aspect at a time,* and to do this, they must eliminate all other aspects and exaggerate or intensify that

43

one. Certain aspects of nature can be presented to us by means of certain painting qualities. The controlling of the light in an object is necessary to the painter if he is to present to us the form of the object, *intensified*.

Form in nature is subject to no change while all the other aspects of it are. Color changes, light changes, but the form of an object remains always the same. Perhaps this is the reason for its being the eternal preoccupation of the serious artist. He attains it either by means of color, or by means of light and shade, as we have seen. Sometimes he attains it by functional line, but that is not properly the method of the painter as much as it is the draughtsman's. Line at best can *represent* form, it cannot create an intensified illusion of it.

There is one other quality closely allied to form. It is the relation of forms to each other, called the *spatial relation*. By means of this quality we are made to feel not only the distance in a picture, but the distance between the various objects in the picture. The artist achieves the same relationship in his picture as in nature. Nature is vast and limitless and a canvas is only a matter of square inches or feet. Yet there have been some artists who have managed to create the illusion of the distance and space between the objects in their canvas so perfectly that we stand before their pictures entranced, feeling ourselves a part of them. We often say in looking at a painting, it looks as if we were gazing out of a window. Spatial relation or space composition, as it is sometimes called, creates this effect.

44

One way of achieving this feeling of distance and space is by means of perspective. Perspective is nothing more than functional line. We have only to draw two converging car tracks on a blank square to get the illusion of distance. We can also create the illusion of distance by diminishing the proportions of objects as they recede. This is indirectly the same principle, as we can see in the sketches below.

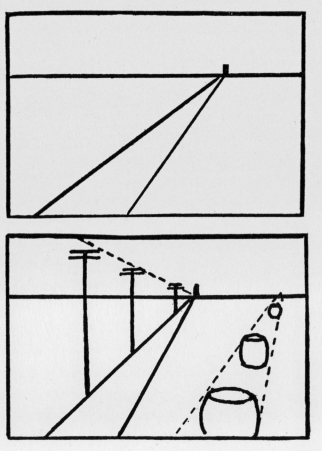

45

The artist is no more content with these simple expedients of line than he is with the substitution of functional line for color and values in securing form. He uses these same qualities to achieve space. He leads us into his picture by making us feel that each object is placed in an atmosphere natural to it alone. We identify the object with the light about it. We therefore identify ourselves with what is real to us. Some artists were masters of putting each mass, whether animate or inanimate, in the exact atmosphere and light pertinent to it. For example, if they had a great stretch of field and a number of haystacks on it scattered at different distances, they would so paint each haystack that it would seem to belong to the one spot in which it was, because the light around it seemed natural to that spot only. This way of painting a mass according to the way it receives the light and is bathed in it is called *architechtonic;* the masses are treated like pieces of architecture. The Florentine painter Perugino was the greatest exponent of architechtonic composition.

Cezanne attempted with much success to attain the same effect, not with light, but with color. He gave each distance and each object the color proper to it alone. His pictures have the power of thrilling us by making us feel that we are looking over a territory of many square miles.

*　　*　　*

THERE remains one attribute to discuss which is essentially more one of the painter than of painting. This quality is

46

8. THE CONCERT—GIORGIONE

10. MOSES STRIKING THE ROCK —
ARTIST UNKNOWN

significance. We spoke before of Van Gogh's significant, original manner of seeing things and of presenting them to us. Significance is really the vitality of the artist. A picture may have all the good qualities of painting in it, but if it is presented to us in a commonplace way, or if the artist saw his subject in a commonplace way, the picture can have no great vitality. The importance of significance may be made clear if we compare it with decoration. When we bow very politely to an acquaintance whom we meet and say, "Did you have a good time over the week-end?" we do not listen to the reply. Our acquaintance realizes that we are observing the social amenities. Our bow is mere decoration, as is the question. What we really mean to say is "hello." But if we ask the same question and wink our eye, the question is fraught with meaning. It is no longer decoration, it takes on significance.

The slightest gesture, pose, or distortion can give a picture significance. The very point of view of the artist may give his picture significance, as we have seen by the way in which Van Gogh looked down upon his chair. A child may draw a picture of a horse, and the rough draw-ing will have significance because it shows us a particular point of view, fresh and unspoiled. He will place the horse in the center of his paper, in the most obvious position, and still the drawing will attract us by its original way of seeing the animal. A grown painter, on the other hand, cannot place his horse in the same obvious position in his canvas,

47

copy the outlines as carefully as the child does, and still give his picture significance, unless his mental development is greatly arrested. The child is original. If the painter imitates the child, he is not original, nor is his picture significant, except possibly psychopathically.

Significance in a picture depends largely on the purpose of the painter. A dramatic scene lacking in drama is a total failure, no matter how well painted. The painter of lion hunts will invest his animals and hunters with all the dynamic action possible. Significance, however, is not necessarily drama. The painter who is interested in the color of a lion's skin can serve his purpose by painting a stuffed lion without dramatic action and still have significance. This quality of a picture, then, depends upon what the subject or scene meant to the artist.

Nevertheless it will become apparent to us, in the course of our survey of painting, that the greatest painters of all time were those who were the keenest psychologists. They were able to awaken and hold the interest of the spectator by means of some novel and pungent observation and statement.

* * *

To summarize the painter's means, then, we have:

A. *Design*

    1. Pattern
       (a) Color
       (b) Value
       (c) Line
    2. Rhythm
       (a) Line

B. *Form*

    1. Functional Line
    2. Planes
       (a) Color
       (b) Value or Chiaroscuro

C. *Spatial Relation*

    1. Functional Line
    2. Color and Value

D. *Significance*

3

AN EXERCISE IN ANALYSIS

❱❱❰❰

IN THIS chapter we shall practice the analysis of paintings. Of the eight pictures reproduced, four have painting qualities or *plastic* qualities, as they are sometimes called, and are therefore *esthetically valid;* the other four are lacking in one or more essentials. The latter are not the worst obtainable; they have been chosen because they are representative of common failings found in their different types, such as the nude, the landscape, etc.

First is a picture of a nude. It is called *The Awakening of*

50

Spring (Fig. 2). The editor of the magazine in which the reproduction appeared, says of it: "This figure study is one of the latest works of the master and is particularly notable, in the canvas itself, for the brilliantly life-like quality of the eyes. The entire composition is one of exceptional beauty."

We must be skeptical of praise. The eyes of the girl are brilliantly life-like, but this in itself constitutes no claim to art. A wax manikin in a store window may have brilliantly life-like eyes, yet the purchasing committee of the Metropolitan Museum does not rush into the manager's office to buy the manikin for the sculpture gallery. We have seen that the Greek artist Zeuxis produced no art when he painted brilliantly life-like grapes that fooled such expert connoisseurs as birds. Life-like brilliance is a trick rather than a quality of art.

Before examining the validity of the editor's statement regarding the exceptional beauty of the composition, let us devote a little time to the artist's point of view. The symbolism, or the conception is not strikingly original, nor in any sense profound. A little chick being hatched out of an egg, a gasoline pump receiving a new coat of paint, in fact any of the usual cartoons would tell the story as effectively. So that rather than possessing significance the point of view is commonplace.

There remains the question of the nude as art. According to the title, the girl was meant to symbolize Spring. But there is no symbolism in the treatment or painting of the

51

girl. She is not a fanciful creature, rather an attractively real girl. That is, her realness approaches a photograph of a real girl. Neither a sprite, nor a fairy, she is a type of urban young lady posed in the nude, made to sit on grass under a tree.

It is plain, then, that the nude as a symbol loses its validity since it is not an allegorical or symbolical figure but a realistic one. We must judge it as a nude, not as a fanciful product of the imagination. To determine then the point of view of the artist is not very difficult, since the pose, or gesture, the smile, the realistic shine in the eyes particularly, make it plain that the painter was not so much interested in lines or forms or abstract qualities as he was in painting the charms of a particular person.

Now since the picture in its conception possesses no significance, and is, besides, false (because the private attitude of the artist is not what his title leads us to expect), is it worth while investigating its claims to art on the ground of its *painting qualities?* For practice let us do so.

"The entire composition is one of exceptional beauty." Composition is another name for design. We have seen that it may be obtained by pattern or by rhythm. Does this picture have pattern? To determine this we turn the picture on its side, or upside down, so that we are not distracted by the meaning of the objects. Do we see anything that corresponds to a map of several states? Only the figure stands out, the rest is smoky, woolly background. The values in the background are confused. No part stands

52

away from the rest. Since we have only one pattern of light against an indeterminate mass of dark, we cannot call this "a variety of shapes, sizes, colors and values."

Perhaps the picture has rhythm. But there is no repetition of line since there is no line to begin with. There is no more rhythm than there is pattern. And so we cannot say with the magazine editor that the entire composition is one of exceptional beauty.

Then there is the matter of form. There is a certain hazy, indistinct suggestion of contour, or outline, but not enough even to substitute for form in painting. No volume or solidity is apparent in the picture. We cannot feel, for instance, that the arms are round, that the body, or torso, has any bulk or weight, that the breasts actually protrude from the body. The whole figure is flat. A figure without form, especially a nude, fails in its purpose. It is disappointing, like a loaf of bread which fails to rise; and it has no more art value than bad currency has monetary value.

As art, then, *The Awakening of Spring* is not a great success. It may give some of us pleasure, but this pleasure will have no relationship to esthetic pleasure. It may suggest all sorts of pleasure, but art must keep our minds upon itself, and not send us off to daydreaming.

In contrast to this, we have a nude called *Bather Arranging Her Hair* (Fig. 3). In it there is no symbolism of a trite and obvious kind, no parables or allegories. It is simple reality. The girl sits on a grassy mound, but she has something under her to keep from catching cold. She is not smiling for the cameraman as is the other nude. She is the impersonal object of the painter's interest. So to begin with, we are not distressed by a cheapness of conception. The picture is objective, just as Van Gogh's portrait of the chair is objective.

Nor is the artist advertising a particular model. He is intensely interested in recording what is before him, but he is not excited, nor does he wish to excite us. If he had wanted to appeal to our burlesque-show emotions, he would not have drawn the left leg as shapeless as if it were in a plaster cast. He has searched out the *abstract* lines and forms.

The picture is well composed. The space in the canvas is well divided into pattern, well organized. The swirling lines of the trees and grass are offset by the more severe lines, round as well as straight, in the figure of the nude. It is true that there is no great inventiveness or originality shown in the arrangement of the background. (Later, in our investigations of the aims of the artist, Renoir, and of the other Post-Impressionist leaders we shall come to see why.) But we must certainly grant that the first requisite, that of organization of space, is present.

It is the form, however, which gives the painting its distinction. Comparatively few artists in the history of painting have been successful in creating the illusion of volume or bulk or roundness in their representations of nudes. The young lady symbolizing the awakening of

54

Spring seems to have been twice gone over by a steam roller. The whole body of the *Bather*, on the other hand, from the foot to the nose and forehead and hair and fingers, is painted with the determined purpose of revealing the form. The arms are firm and round. The breasts are as convincingly round as they would be in a piece of sculpture. The illusion is achieved by a severe but subtle restraint of the light in each form. In the Spring picture the nude is flat because the light is diffused. There is no attempt to control it and use it in the one place that will best suggest the form. Compare the hip, for instance, with the hip of the *Bather*. In the latter the light is kept in the center with the result that the part appears as round and as solid as a watermelon.

In addition to the composition and the form, there is the design in the figure itself. This is largely a matter of the pose. The pose is made to reveal rhythmic lines.

Rhythms are the most important means for the sculptor to achieve design. A statue has no background except the park or garden or public square in which it eventually finds itself. Unless the sculptor is a landscape artist as well, he must confine his design to his figure. He must pose his model in such a way that the lines, *repeating each other at intervals,* give a unified expression to the figure. He cannot have all his lines running in different directions because it would destroy the meaning he wishes to give to the figure. Instead of being unified it would be disconnected and chaotic. So he will make the angle of the neck,

55

let us say, repeat the angle of the forearm, etc. When you consider that a statue must be interesting from every side, you see how much greater the problem of rhythm in a figure is to the sculptor than to the painter. Yet few painters are artists enough to devise a pose that possesses rhythm.

Look once more at *The Awakening of Spring*. The curves of the arms, posed like an orchestra conductor's, are totally unrelated to anything else in the figure. No other lines repeat them. In Renoir's nude, on the other hand, the girl's right arm follows the direction of her right leg. The left arm from the elbow to the shoulder repeats the bottom line of the thigh. The left leg and the left side of the abdomen are parallel. These repetitions create a harmony and grace.

Restful stability is given to the figure of the *Bather* by the device of putting two lights in the grass at the bottom of the canvas, one on each side leading up to the torso of the girl. The result is a triangle or base upon which the figure appears to be resting, much as a statuette rests upon a base. The other nude lacks this stability, threatening to topple over to the left.

The difference between the two nudes we see is vast. But the important thing is that the painter of the second one regarded his nude as a real flesh and blood young woman and proceeded to present her to us as such. He did not make a literal copy which would have been meaningless and uninteresting but he invented, arranged, and

56

stressed certain aspects of truth, notably the form. He made these truths appealing, not the young lady.

If he had chosen to paint a sprite or nymph or other fanciful creature he no doubt would have painted her less realistically, more in accordance with the demands of the imagination. The Florentine painter Botticelli painted women who were fanciful and not real. Their beauty is no whit less than that of the real. They were consistent with the artist's intention or attitude.

Now let us turn our attention to the next picture, *The Golden Wedding Anniversary* (Fig. 4). Different in subject from the last picture, it is also different in its qualities. It has, to some slight degree, an arrangement of line and space. If we turn it upside down, for instance, we can find in it shapes and sizes that are different from each other. There is some pattern. But since most of the picture is taken up with the two figures, the quality of the painting will naturally depend upon them. Do they possess form? Do the parts of the face protrude and recede as they do in nature? No, they are done like photographs. They are only photographic records of lights and shadows just as they happen at the moment. Solidity, the result of restrained use of light, is therefore absent. We are made to feel only the *story* of the picture, the anecdote. This is an example of an illustration in the technique of a painting. By placing the old man with an arm about his devoted wife, and a bouquet of flowers in his hand, the artist, or illustrator,

57

makes a bid for our sympathy. Nice old duck, we say. To think that these two have been married for fifty years and are still smiling.

We have seen that this illustration is not art since the painting itself does not hold our interest more than the story. The *motive* of the artist was not so much to produce a fine painting as to sell us the sentiment or the idea of marital felicity by means of a painted anecdote. The anecdote comes first, the painting is secondary.

The reverse is true of the picture *The Two Clowns* (Fig. 5). Daumier, who painted this picture, was regarded during his lifetime as an ironic commentator on the foibles and injustices of his period. The term artist was not applied to him. His powerful draughtsmanship carried so much meaning that critics themselves were blinded to the art qualities in the man. It is only recently that they have come to give him his due.

His preoccupation with stories would naturally manifest itself in his "fine art." The picture of one clown whispering to another in the wings of a stage is as literary as the *Golden Wedding* anecdote which we found banal illustration. Like the *Golden Wedding*, it starts us off on the manufacture of a story. "Pipe the dame in the lower box to the right," whispers the clown in black. "Um, *pas mal*," says the one in white leeringly. *"Quel embonpoint!"*

But compare the two pictures for art qualities. In this picture of the clowns you have, in contrast to the Golden Wedding, strikingly original pattern. The light mass in

58

the upper right corner of the canvas comes down in a definite shape to the white collar of the clown. This white collar "ties up" with the white cuff and the white hand, the little finger of which points to the ear of the clown whose face fascinates us. Thus we are led from one side of the canvas, by the force of the light and the direction of the line, to the important focal point. The white belt or sash at the lower right also leads us swiftly, by means of the patterns of white collar points, to the same place. So surely is our eye carried to the center of interest that unless something massive were in the composition to stop it, our glance would be swirling without rest. As it is, the artist has thrown a great mass of light at a sharp angle against the little finger—the immovable body stops the irresistible force. The black triangular mass of the clown on the right gives the canvas a further balance. The feeling of stability affects us much as a well-designed mass of sculpture does.

The strength of the composition is further enhanced by the simple, powerful painting of the heads. The flat, photographic heads in the *Golden Wedding* are weak in comparison to the clowns. The artist has done his utmost to remove from the faces any detail which adds nothing to their significance. In his efforts to drive home his story he has dramatically overstated the facts, particularly in exaggerating the size of the eyes. This is the painter's use of distortion, which will be discussed in greater detail later.

The form of the figures is sculptural. Due to the odd lighting, the artist has resorted to functional line to strengthen his modeling. An example of this device is found in the neck of the clown in black. But its judicious use detracts nothing from the value of the work.

All in all, this canvas, which could easily have been a mere cartoon or illustration, embodies the qualities of art. It has strength, simplicity, originality of pattern, and an unmatched economy of means. It has excellent form and graceful rhythm. (If we half close our eyes, for example, we see how the shadow below the collar of the clown in white repeats the white semicircle below the neck of the other clown.)

We come now to another type of picture. This, like the *Golden Anniversary*, aims to sell us a sentiment, or to awaken in us thoughts completely foreign to the painting itself. It is called *Moonlight on the Lake* (Fig. 6). It would be difficult for the greatest painter of all time, whoever he may be, to tackle such a subject and make art out of it. The handicap is too great. The very sound of the words sets us to daydreaming of our distant, romantic youth.

Besides, the nature of the subject automatically eliminates one painting quality, color. All colors must be subordinated to the color of night. This is not to say that all nocturnes have no art value, but that in order for a nocturne to have art value, the other qualities must compensate for the absence of color.

Do we find such compensation? Is the composition so

exceptional that we are fascinated by its inventiveness and variety? On the contrary, the picture is too evenly divided in area, in the size of its masses, or shapes, to have much interest for us on the score of pattern. There is pattern, but it is uninteresting, uninventive, lacking in originality. It is the kind of pattern any student is capable of achieving.

Does the picture have form? Spatial relation? It is as flat as a landscape in a theater backdrop. A landscape can have form, just as well as a barrel or a bottle. Cezanne's landscapes leap and swell with form. We shall examine one presently and see how the Frenchman accomplished it. But in the moonlight picture the trees are flat and .throughout there is an absence of solidity and space and distance. Plainly the artist was not intent upon attaining qualities. Rather it appears that he was carried away by romantic sentiment and wished to transfer it to us.

Of course this moonlight picture is an illustration. It is *literary*, that is, it gives us a starting point for a story and we set off to fabricate the story. It could be told in words much better than in pictures. The quiet splendor of nightfall on the dank lagoon. In the distance come the strains of the Blue Danube Waltz. Cinderella lies languid in the silvery bark, while her fairy prince, etc.

To people who have difficulty in visualizing from a writer's words, pictures like the *Moonlight* are a great boon. But to those of us who prefer our romance in a more real world there can be no doubt that the picture is commonplace in conception, an invitation to daydreaming.

61

Now let us turn to a valid landscape such as Cezanne's painting, *Sainte Victoire* (Fig. 7).

First we shall examine the design. Turning it upon its side it does not seem to have any pattern at all. But it really possesses as much design as a Persian rug. Instead of being divided into masses, its pattern is attained by rhythms. There are whole series of lines, curved and straight, which follow each other. If this were a piece of cretonne and not an oil painting each series of lines would be called a *motif*. It is interesting to note that while the designer of textiles experiments until he hits upon a pleasing combination of motifs, the artist in painting from nature instinctively selects *from nature* the lines and accents of dark and light which will grace his picture through their rhythms. Here is a fine example of design attained by rhythm.

Besides good design, the picture has exceptional spatial relation. This is achieved by planes. When you open your hands and hold them upright, little fingers together, they are both on one plane. But if you place one hand a little behind the other, and then a little more, and then still more, each time the hand moves back it is on another plane. In the *Moonlight* there is no feeling of one part of the picture being on a different plane from the rest. And for that reason it is flat. Cezanne's picture seems to have as many planes as nature itself. The foliage of the tree in the foreground is thick and voluminous. The little house in the lower left has sides and top on different planes.

62

11. FRAGMENT OF GREEK VASE

12. CHRIST—UNKNOWN BYZANTINE ARTIST

The mountains swell as if they were inflated. Each meadow seems vast in itself. The illusion of vastness and extent in a small canvas is convincingly attained. Unfortunately we cannot show the original painting to explain his novel method. For he accomplished this feat of spatial relation not by resorting to strong light and shade (or a tremendous range of values), but by means of his own invention of using a warm color next to a cold one, that is to say, using colors having red and yellow predominant in them, next to colors in which blue and green and crimson predominate. This is without doubt a most effective means and explains why art students stand before his pictures like ancient pilgrims before the Oracle of Delphi.

There remains only one aspect of the painting to mention. That is the point of view from which it was approached. While the *Moonlight* picture is romantic, sentimental, the *Sainte Victoire* landscape holds us *in* the picture by the form, the spatial relation, the decorative beauty of the lines and rhythms, and by the apparent preoccupation of the artist in striving for these qualities. He is not emotional and does not wish to make us so. He is objective.

A different type of picture from those already discussed is the group portrait. The *Homage to Delacroix* (Fig. 8) is a painting similar to the hundreds of group pictures we have seen in banks, universities, medical societies, etc. This type of picture originated long before the advent of the camera— probably when the first Italian acquired sufficient money and self-esteem to commission an artist to do the whole

63

family in one canvas. During the Renaissance it enjoyed its greatest vogue. Veronese painted acres of group portraits. The purpose was chiefly to preserve for posterity the images of a group prominent in the community.

Now we have the camera. There is no longer any need for stringing six heads in the upper row and four heads in the lower, with a framed head in the top center. Or if there is, the interest is purely historical, or antiquarian. There may be good reasons for having such pictures, but they are reasons removed from art.

As the painter's art, the picture will not stand the test of our inquisition. We see that the arrangement is monotonous, lacking in inventiveness, unoriginal. The faces and figures are treated photographically. But the picture has more interest for us than the other poor ones we have examined, in that it is at least painted objectively.

The artist has attempted to present accurately the persons in the picture. He has given us his humble, honest efforts. He has fallen short of art, because he was too much concerned with copying instead of organizing what was before him in such a way that we would be shown a new point of view, something fresh and vital.

But in fairness to the painter of this present group we must not put him in the ranks of the shallow portrait craftsmen. He has, at least, spared us that aggressive facility and cleverness which was brought into vogue in the last century by Carolus-Duran and which culminated in his famous pupil, Sargent. None of these eleven noses

64

was painted in three strokes. There is no virtuosity of the brush that whirls our eyes around as a cat plays with a mouse. This artist, if too literal, at least respects our person.

A far more successful attempt at portrait grouping is shown in *The Concert* (Fig. 9), painted by the Venetian Giorgione some three hundred years before the *Homage to Delacroix*. The motif of this composition is the triangle. The figure in the center is the most important one. He is a large black triangular mass. His neck is triangular. His face is triangular. The part of the piano which is visible is a triangle. The musician on the right holding the cello is divided into triangles, all except his head. His head is round, as is the head of the young person on the left. These round heads stop the action in the picture. The triangles build the composition up to the center head. They lead our glance to it. To keep it there, our eyes are fastened in by the round, static forms just as a sentence is fastened in by a period before it and after it. The dynamic action of the triangle is brought to a halt. Note how the figure on the left is cut into a triangle, but how the round line of the forehead and the plume of the hat effectively keep our gaze from shooting out of the picture.

The result of this triangular arrangement is that we are not the least bit disturbed by the fact that there are three heads in a row. Looking back at the other group portrait, we see that the vapidity of the thing is due to a lack of geometric design. The heads are regimented across the picture like soldiers on parade. When we have looked from left to right we have exhausted the canvas. In *The Concert*, on the other hand, our gaze is started circulating from one pattern to another, to rest finally upon the most interesting face, that of the pianist. When we have finished looking we begin again. The excellence of the design may overshadow the form in the picture, but it is enough to note that the faces seem carved of marble.

*　　*　　*

FORTIFIED with this experience at analysis, we shall begin in the next chapter a brief outline of the origins and aims of painting, confining our examinations henceforth to the most interesting examples of each period and country. We shall see how inevitable it was for painting to grow into the Modernism we find about us.

PART TWO

❯❯❯·❯❯❯·❮❮·❮❮

The Development of Painting

4

ART BEFORE GIOTTO

-»»-»»-«««-

HISTORIES of European painting usually begin with Giotto. If we were concerned only or especially with the lives of the great masters we should do the same. But since our interest is in the art of painting, and in the changes in the point of view of artists, we must go beyond Giotto to the earliest artistic efforts of the Christian Primitives.

It is commonly believed that European artists of the second, third and fourth centuries were clumsy and crude; we are taught to smile with indulgence upon the childish conceptions and execution of the frescoes that have been found in the Christian catacombs. But we forget that this naïve, unskillful art is the work, not of the artists of the period, but of preachers untrained in drawing and painting. The zealous converts took upon themselves the task of first illustrating the Scriptures, just as today ladies on the entertainment committees of churches will often make the signs and posters for strawberry festivals, instead of hiring professional sign painters to do the work.

The real artists of early Rome, which ruled all civilized Europe, were in the employ of the rich. Not only were pagan temples decorated with frescoes, sculpture-reliefs, altar pieces and countless images of gods, but the lordly government officials vied with each other in the decorative magnificence of their homes. Artists are notoriously indifferent to religious quarrels and activities, the psychologists attributing their detachment to the fact that art is itself a religion with them—the worship of beauty; so the fervid zeal of the Christians found few converts among painters and sculptors. There was little chance of inducing a successful, talented artist to forsake the honors, rewards, and admiration of the leading classes, in order to paint the pictures or carve the altar pieces of a hunted and hated body of poor zealots (who, moreover, were by training and condition unfitted to experience a proper appreciation of art, which is to the artist almost as precious as his bread).

So the task of telling the stories of the Bible fell to the preachers or to the artisans and skilled mechanics among

70

the converts. They made up in passionate sincere feeling what they lacked in knowledge of proportions and design and anatomy. And the lack of any artistic tradition behind their work gave it a kind of originality that has served to amuse numbers of cynics. We cannot, unfortunately, compare their crude and sincere efforts with the polished art of the pagan temples, since, in the sudden overwhelming ascendancy of Christianity in the third and fourth centuries, the Roman houses of worship and all their art were destroyed by mobs of rioting believers of the new faith. (The Christians were intent upon serving their lately acquired God and the bishops by destroying all vestiges of an immoral competition.) We may see, however, what a superior art, from the point of view of decorative skill and knowledge, the art of the pagans was, by looking at the frescoes unearthed at Pompeii, mercifully (and paradoxically) saved from destruction by burial under the lava of volcanic eruptions.

Yet we must confess that the untrained art of the early Christians moves us, in a different way of course, equally as much as the finer art of the pagan artists. There is a vitality of spirit and an emotional honesty seldom found in the more decorative work. The amateurs succeeded in instilling into their paintings something of the essence of the new religion. The spirit was stressed, not the decorative forms. The inability to draw and paint a graceful, ideal figure served, instead of hampered, the humble and pious

71

preachers in conveying to the spectator the moral lessons of the Bible.

In order to show the difference between the art of the early Christians of Rome which was, as we have said, a sincere but amateur art, and the decorative art of the professional painters of the pagans, we reproduce a fresco of early Christian art found in the catacombs (Fig. 10), and a fragment of a Greek vase of some seven hundred years earlier (Fig. 11). The fresco represents Moses striking the rock. The figures are ludicrous in drawing and proportion, yet if we look at them for a time we are affected by the simplicity and singleness of idea in the presentation. There is little art but much clarity of message, like a child's drawing, or like hieroglyphics. The Greek painting depicts a combat between the gods and the giants. It is merely decoration, beautiful in pattern, correct in drawing, skillfully executed. But it might just as well be called The Horse Fair. The spirit is missing. We are not made to feel that there is any combat going on. Turning to the Biblical illustration, we see that the crude efforts of the amateur were the first steps in the establishment of a new art which lacked the decorative principles of the professionals but which affects us through its single-minded intensity.

The most noteworthy thing about this early Christian art is that its defective drawing and proportions *became symbolic of Christianity*. The Christians at first were the poor and the hunted whose only pleasure came in the contemplation of a future life. They were of necessity

72

ascetics. The pleasures of the pagans were to them anathema. An art which represented a human being who was homely and even ugly was more suited to their spiritual faith than an art which delighted in showing man and woman as finely proportioned animals. So that even when there was sufficient talent among them to enable them to have their Biblical characters as good looking as the gods of the pagans, they exhibited a preference for the ill-proportioned, ascetic images as symbols of their faith.

This asceticism in Christian art is best exemplified in the art of the Byzantines. Asia Minor was early converted to the new religion, but it was centuries before there was established a church organization comparable to that at Rome. So that there is an interval of a few hundred years between the art of the catacombs and the mosaics and altar pieces of the Byzantines. There is a decidedly Oriental flavor to the latter: a sense of ornament which has remained unsurpassed for richness and inventiveness. This decorative skill shows the influence of the Chinese, in the treatment of landscape, and of the Persians in color and in pattern. There is no reason to suppose that the Byzantine artists were inferior in draughtsmanship to the ancient Greeks, yet their figures of Biblical characters, especially that of Christ, are painted in an almost hideous distortion apparently for the purpose of causing the spectator to shudder in sympathy. Their paintings, however, soon became stylized; for instance, the lines expressing the sorrow

73

of a face were treated as symmetrical design. The reproduction illustrates this tendency (Fig. 12).

Pagan art and pagan religion, essentially decorative,
never concerned themselves with human anguish. They
made physical life pleasurable—but only for those privi-
leged to enjoy it. Opposed to this creed of lust, rituals,
joyous energy, Christianity aimed at solace for the unhappy, the excluded. It opened new fields of spiritual
pleasure for the physically oppressed. Art is turned from a
purely objective or decorative pursuit to the rendering of
human service. The artist conveys the *thoughts and visions
and feelings* calculated to uplift the spirit. These thoughts
and feelings are not dependent upon systems of decoration
or other conventional means. They come from the imaginative mind and the fervent heart. In other words, we have
in Christian painting the birth of *subjective* art.

For centuries painting in Europe remained in its
amateur status. There were no doubt many itinerant
artisans who lived by the profession of illustration for
churches but on the whole the artisan of talent found more
lucrative work in the applied arts. It was not until the
Church had attained a degree of power and wealth that
gave it a dominant position in State affairs that it was
able to attract men of creative ability (generally Byzantines), and cause to spring up schools for professional
artists. Rigid geometric design stamps this era of Primitive painting, not to be confused with the earlier art of

74

the Martyrs. One of the outstanding teachers of this period, the thirteenth century, was Cimabue.

His work clearly shows the Byzantine influence (Fig. 13) He used gold leaf for the halos about the heads of his saints and angels, a procedure which was almost a precept of Byzantine art. His arches, columns and architectural ornament were likewise derived from Asia Minor. Only his faces and costumes are Italian. But his painting, while more realistic, is also less vital, less religiously spirited—a kind of indeterminate compromise between Oriental design and illustration of his surroundings. His work is important historically, but actually it leaves us cold.

There is nothing spiritual in the faces of his Madonnas, angels and prophets. While the tilt of the head or the gesturing hands and arms are meant to indicate some emotion, the faces are devoid of expression. They are not interesting either as painting or character portrayal. When we compare them to the faces painted by Greek artists twelve or fifteen hundred years earlier, we see what little progress had been made in the art of portraiture. We reproduce two portraits found wrapped up with mummies (Fig. 14). Although they make no pretensions to character analysis and are as objective as possible, we find that the simple representation holds us by its honesty as well as by its peculiar technique. Without any religious motive to assist him the Greek artist has put much greater character into his faces than has the mediæval one.

Yet Cimabue's work, as we said, is interesting historically. The very lifelessness or realistic vapidity of his figures is sufficient indication of a change in religious attitude that was creeping into early Italian society. Christianity was no longer the hope of the downtrodden and the defeated; it was beginning to hold up its head. It was casting off asceticism. It was looking at the things of this world, not of the next. Not until the Renaissance, a hundred and fifty years later, did it completely emerge as a pleasurable, decorative, pagan sort of faith. But the first warnings of the change were visible in the unrealized efforts of this Florentine Primitive, Cimabue.

Cimabue was born in 1240 and died in 1301. The condition of Florentine society in his day throws as much light upon him as his pictures do upon the changing ideals of his compatriots. In the latter part of the thirteenth century, Italy was already renowned for its cultural advancement over the rest of Europe. The French philosopher Taine draws a vivid picture of the times, contrasting the high civilization of Italy with the barbarous warring races of the north who lived in brutality and ignorance. Historians of the period describe vividly the interest of the Florentine nobles and citizens in the works of the architects, painters, sculptors and poets. Charles of Anjou, more appreciative of art than most of his countrymen of that period, found in Florence an environment to his regal taste. On one of his visits he was so thrilled by the art of Cimabue, that, accompanied by his lords and ladies, he marched in procession with the citizens and their trumpeters, from the studio of the artist to the Church of Santa Maria Novella where "the largest altar piece yet painted" was to be installed.

We note here that the general interest in art was accompanied by a certain materialistic urge for pomp and splendor. The Church encouraged these tendencies. The stage is already set for the Renaissance. There were, of course, certain direct causes which brought about the sudden lush productivity of art that amazed the world. But we must avoid the popular error that Cimabue and his fellow Primitives who painted such droll canvases lived in an unorganized society, among barbarous illiterates, who at the year 1450 suddenly went artistic, thus producing a Renaissance. The cultural soil was already there, it only remained for the genius to plant the seed which was later to flourish so richly. Giotto was that genius.

5

GIOTTO AND FRA ANGELICO

❯❯❯·❯❯❯·❮❮❮·❮❮❮

IN ACTUAL time only a few years separate Giotto from Cimabue. Vasari, the historian of Florence, tells the touching story of how the renowned Cimabue, strolling out into the country, came upon the youngster scraping upon a rock the outlines of one of the sheep which he had been set to watch, and how the master had been so delighted with the boy's talent that he had immediately arranged to bring him to Florence as his pupil. But more accurate historians, with no cause to be overpatriotic for beloved

Florence, have rejected this story as fable. In view of the innovations in painting effected by Giotto and his completely different point of view, it seems more reasonable to suppose that his talents were unspoiled by his celebrated predecessor.

Nature and the high degree of the culture of the time coöperated to produce in Giotto exceptional talents. He was a genius. A close friend of the immortal Dante, he was himself no mean poet. And so renowned was he for his wit and his spirited conversation that many distinguished Florentines sought him for their social gatherings. In a day when guests never had cause to fear the banalities of after-dinner speeches he was an outstanding attraction. As a sculptor he ranks with the best of his time. And as an architect alone he would have achieved sufficient distinction to earn him a place in the history of art. Whoever has seen the Duomo in Florence will acknowledge his mastery of architectural design. He was a genius, but not, as some historians have it, a phenomenon. Gentle Italy, which had tamed the invading barbarians of the north, and which was to produce the great Leonardo, bred and fostered scores of well-rounded, talented men decades before the Renaissance. It was in Giotto's innovations, in his new point of view, in his scientific discoveries, as well as in his great spiritual and poetic resources that he established himself as one of the most important painters of all time.

Like Cimabue, he is called a Primitive. But some critics, notably Berenson, include him in their discussions of

Renaissance art. The difference between the Primitives and the painters of the Renaissance is the difference in the religious point of view. The Primitives, like the early Christian amateur artists of the catacombs, stressed the *spiritual*, the *subjective*, the emotional side of religion. Their work was characterized by a rigid and sometimes involved system of design derived from the Byzantines, of whom there were many itinerant representatives in Italy. We shall see that the Renaissance painters, on the other hand, were concerned, as were the ancient Greeks and the pagan Romans, primarily with the beauty of the human body, the physical ideal; and that their pictures are characterized by a reality, a scientific understanding, a warmth of color and a general plausibility never before realized. In other words, their art was something completely opposed in spirit to the asceticism and subjectivity of the Primitives. The cult of self-denial, humility, the flagellation of the spirit, the smell of monasteries, were forgotten by the adventurous, joyous Christians who made a great to-do about the paintings of the stories of the Bible, but whose concepts of life were thoroughly pagan.

While Giotto remains in spirit a Primitive, in execution he anticipates the Golden Era. He was the first European painter to shake off the traditions of the Byzantines and paint objects and people with some scientific understanding of the problems of perspective and form and light and shade. He makes his figures appear real instead of reducing them to a conventional system of design and depending

80

upon morbid distortion and emaciation to drive home the lesson of Christian humility. His scenes are simple and plausible, yet they are bathed in an atmosphere of mysticism. This combining of the real with the imagined, or if we prefer, the objective with subjective, gives him a unique place in the history of painting. He is the link between the Primitives and the painters of the Renaissance.

Being an innovator at a time when innovation in painting was an event of importance and not the result of a search for novelty at the cost of everything else, Giotto's work was considered sensational. It was not generally understood since he was, in knowledge and scientific observation, far ahead of his time. While many painters were fascinated by his canvases, few grasped his principles and the value of his restrained dramatic force; and since most painters are mere craftsmen, his contemporaries succeeded only in copying the *surface effects* and the technique. The combination of his grasp upon the qualities of painting and his poetic manner of presentation was something that baffled his hosts of followers and imitators.

To realize how far ahead of his time he was, we have only to compare one of his earliest paintings, *The Death of Saint Francis* (Fig. 15), painted long before the full attainment of his powers, with a similar composition, *The Death of Saint Jerome* (Fig. 16), painted a century later by Sano di Pietro.

Let us look first at the Saint Jerome. The picture is highly ornamented with gold leaf, pressed into different decorative *motifs* in the Byzantine manner. The halos are not only gold, they are as fancy as a Mexican chieftain's saddle. The figures of the friars are all short with large heads, a tradition which dates back to the earliest Christian art such as our picture of Moses striking the rock. In the paintings of the heads the only imagination shown is in the different decorative treatments of the beards; otherwise, the monks may be taken for brothers as well as Fathers. Grief is depicted in each face in precisely the same way, a pulling together of the eyebrows.

The bed upon which the dead Saint Jerome lies seems badly constructed; the slightest push would send it crashing to the floor. And if we look under it we fail to see the lower parts of the Father in black and of the two friars who are bent over the dead man. With the greatest naïveté the artist has cut off their bodies where they cease to be visible at the top. Plainly this is an unconvincing picture, lacking in plausibility. When we consider that there is an almost complete absence of form, and no knowledge of perspective evident in the drawings of the buildings, we see how primitive this painting is.

Yet it does possess a highly meritorious painting quality. As a composition it is not only successful but excellent. The distribution of the black patterns, their different shapes and sizes, all confined to the upper part of the picture so that our gaze is kept circulating around the faces of the friars, is skillfully managed. The figure in black brings our roving glance to a halt. From his black

82

13. MADONNA – CIMABUE

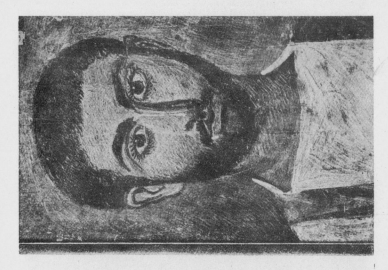

gown we look to the head of the kneeling monk below him, and follow the curved arm of the dead Saint to his holy head. The heavy band of gold which decorates the bed or bier at the bottom, serves to emphasize the importance of the Saint, to *underscore* him. Altogether it is strong composition.

But when we compare this painting with the Giotto, we realize at once all its other limitations. The first thing that strikes us in the Giotto is the manner in which the delegation of monks has been broken up into groups. Instead of ranging them in monotonous formation around the bier, the more ingenious artist has distributed them with the skill of a stage director who wished to shake us with grief. At the foot is the group which the ritual of the Church demands be stationed with the Cross. At the head are the friars who chant for the soul of the Dead. In contrast to these rigid, formally arranged groups, the other friars are in such a state of grief and tension that the emotion is immediately imparted to us. This dramatic *mise-en-scène* in painting is the significance upon which we dwelt in Chapter 2.

We recall that the primitive ascetics, the Byzantines, played upon the emotions of spectators by horrifying them with repulsive distortion, by caricaturing the miserable aspects of creatures writhing in humility; by fancy gold halos about the heads of emaciated saints. And there is no doubt that these means succeeded, because they were intended to impress simple, uncultured people. But Giotto's

83

method, less elementary, was more convincing to a civilized populace.

In actual painting qualities Giotto is as far ahead of his predecessors as in his manner of presentation. Plausibility as we have said, takes the place of decorative conventions. The bed is solid, there is no danger of some one brushing by it and taking off a leg. The banner below the cross sags in the most natural manner. The friars are not manikins cast in a mold with one set of features and one fixed facial expression, but are individual humans, gesturing each in his own way, their bodies bent into different positions. Even in the figures kneeling before the bier, the artist has bothered to show how feet may be caught in long gowns.

Significance and plausibility are not the extent of his innovations. His color is also his own. Instead of the areas of gold, the brilliant deep reds and blues of Oriental design, he preferred to paint his pictures in a light, harmonious palette. Nature, at least in Italy, did not reveal itself to him in brilliant deep colors.

He also discarded the proportions of the Primitives. We see in this *Death of Saint Francis* men of normal build, much better looking than the short, large-headed types generally depicted. The young friars are even handsome. This alone was a departure from custom.

More important than all these changes is Giotto's discovery of the means of expressing form. By a subtle, masterful use of light and shade, he attained a volume and a solidity since unsurpassed. His figures and surfaces are sculptural. He omitted the many details that would encroach upon the simplicity of his forms, as he would if he were carving them from rock. There is a ponderableness to all his figures. To see how simply he realized this quality of form, let us look carefully at a head of Christ in the famous fresco at Padua (Fig. 17). The eyes are in their sockets. The nose comes forward. The forehead is round. There are millions of portraits more clever in brushwork, more luscious in color, but how many of them possess this elementary form? Add to this the poetic conception of Christ, and we see the reasons for Giotto's supreme position in the history of early Italian art.

It was a hundred years after him that a painter appeared who showed talent of as high an order, and who profited by the lessons of the great Florentine. This man was Massaccio. He gave the movement toward the Renaissance an added push by his attention to the problems of figure painting and his complete orientation from the naïve and severe art of the Primitives. But before going on to the new era we may tarry to look at the work of the last of the great Primitives, Fra Beato Angelico.

He is still the religious mystic. It is told of him that he prayed each time before he commenced a painting; that when he depicted the trials of Christ he would be overcome by his tears, and be compelled to leave off working. He was renowned for his goodness and kindness of heart. He was one of the last Christians of the old school who were being fast displaced by converts to the pagan Christianity of gorgeous ritual and pomp.

Looking at his *Flight into Egypt* (Fig. 18), we are struck with the swirling composition of the landscape. It imparts an emotional, subjective atmosphere to the painting. The whole canvas from the rigid unnatural little trees to the decorative grasses in the foreground is unrealistic, the product of a visionary mystic. The scene is not in nature but in the mind. It is truly primitive in feeling, aspiring to God, humble and naïve. The faces of the Madonna and Child are perhaps too sweet and angelic, but otherwise there is an honesty in the painting of the forms, of the animal and of the humans, equally as fine as Giotto's. There is less of the dramatic here than in Giotto's work, but greater emotional intensity, more the painting of the heart. Critics have called it sentimental, but it seems to us the consummation of Primitive art.

6

THE RENAISSANCE IN FLORENCE

❊❊❊❊

WHILE FRA ANGELICO, living in monastic confine-
ment alone with his dreams, painted the Christian soul, the
urge for a more physically wholesome and active existence
was already being reflected in the pictures of other artists.
As if Italy had been for centuries in a state of mourning
and penance, she now cast off her black robes of inhibi-
tions. A sensuous race could not forever be solemn and
subdued. A cultured race could not forever turn its energies
to the flagellation of the spirit. Because Italy was sensu-

ous and cultured and brimful of repressed energy, she threw herself into the proper business of life, enjoyment. It was an awakening of the spirit, the rebirth of the activities and ideals of ancient Greece—the Renaissance.

The rest of Europe did not take part in this dance of life. We have seen that even in the time of Cimabue and Giotto, Italy was far ahead of her neighbors in civilization. Taine in his *Philosophy of Art* contrasts Italian life at the time of the Renaissance with conditions in England, Germany and France. He shows us that at the moment Italy was entering upon its richest era, England was engaged in its horrible War of Roses, in which, the battles over, the children of the vanquished were slaughtered in cold blood. Until the year 1550, England remains a country of hunters, serfs and soldiers. In the interior of the Kingdom only two or three houses in the villages possess chimneys. The homes of country gentlemen are straw-covered huts roughly plastered with mud. The middle classes sleep upon round logs for pillows. The cooking utensils of the house are not even of tin, but of wood.

Germany too is engaged in atrocious warfare. The emperor is without authority; the individual barons, ignorant and insolent, settle their quarrels in their own way, which is by the strength of their fists. The gentlemen and so-called learned class are a coarse and drunken people, if one is to believe the memoirs of Hans of Schweinichen.

As for France, that country is in its most disastrous period in history—conquered and devastated by the Eng-

88

lish. Wolves range through the streets of Paris. And even after the English are driven out, the country is at the mercy of its lords and gentlemen, brigands and assassins who terrify the peasants. The legend of Bluebeard sprang from the escapades of one of these noble murderers, Gilles de Retz. Rabelais more ably than other commentators shows us the bestiality of Gothic customs of the middle of the sixteenth century.

In short, throughout the rest of Europe, the feudal régime still exists. Men are like animals, savage and strong, thinking only of drinking, eating, fighting, and amusing themselves. Italy, on the contrary, is a country almost modern. The Italians manufacture, trade, and spend the money they earn in a civilized manner. The cares of war do not hang over the citizens of Florence. The state employs a system whereby its little battles are fought by paid troops. And these skirmishes seldom amount to war but come to an end with one or two casualties. Everywhere diplomacy attempts to replace force.

Taine tells us of this age of culture and learning. Poets wrote in a Latin as impeccable as that of Cicero and Vergil. Education and erudition were taken out of cloistered monasteries and furthered by princes. Cosimo de Medici founded an academy of philosophy. Princes surrounded themselves with writers, philosophers, artists, in order to converse with them on matters of the spirit. The principal banker of Florence, Lorenzo de Medici, was also one of the principal poets. Cellini tells us that when his statue of

Perseus was unveiled, no less than twenty sonnets were written about it the first day. It is obvious that the society of the period was ripe for a reign of art similar to that of the ancient Greeks.

On the other hand, the individual in this cultivated society does not live in fat security. If there is diplomacy, there is also intrigue. If there is national peace there is much violence in the personal quarrels and encounters of a people of hot blood. The meekness imposed by Christianity has worn off and exposed the natural man; so that we find the cultured sixteenth century Italian primitive and fierce in temperament. The most profound philosophers, such as Machiavelli, carefully reasoned the necessities for treachery, murder and betrayal. The destruction of one's enemies became as fine an art as the painting of altar-pieces for churches. The hero of the period is Cæsar Borgia, the greatest traitor of all time. So necessary for the maintenance of peace did this princely assassin consider dissimulation, perfidy, traps of every device, that he practiced them upon everybody, even his own family. When a noble served him well by carrying out his orders to harass and bleed the people, he had him butchered and exposed in the market place, to show his dear citizens how he dealt with those who oppressed them.

The result of this lack of personal security and police protection was that individuals had to depend upon themselves for attack and defense. They had to acquire the habit of extreme and sudden resolution; which is to say,

90

15. DEATH OF ST. FRANCIS—GIOTTO

Courtesy Anderson, Rome

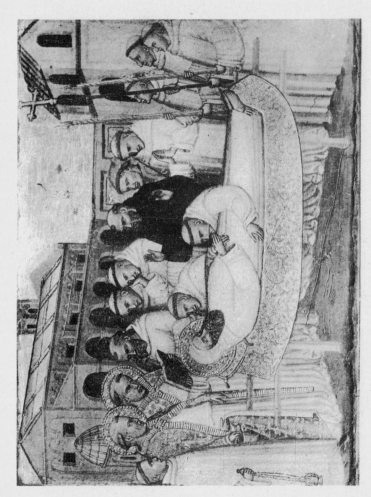

16. DEATH OF ST. JEROME—DI PIETRO

they had to know how to kill and have killed. A man could not be a good, pious, contemplative Christian in such an environment of violence and betrayal. He could not adopt an Oriental attitude of resignation, and still live. He was compelled to be a man of action. The development of the individual into a resourceful man of action is, according to Taine, one of the chief causes for the Renaissance.

We have an excellent example of the nature of such a man in Benvenuto Cellini. His memoirs tell us of the hazards of life, and the resolute and wily efforts of man to overcome them. His own character is distinguished by its energy and courage, its vigorous initiative, its habitude of sudden resolve, its capacity for action and suffering. He was the superb animal, all militant, and all resistant, nourished by the tough customs of medieval society. He was completely masculine. In him was the perfect example of creative ability resulting from wide and active experience and capacity for living.

Physical activity, the necessity for strength and dexterity, brought about an age of athletes similar to the ancient Greeks. Men were proud of their bodies. Exercises and tournaments assumed a great importance. The handsome athletic body was as much a public ideal as it had been in pagan times. The slim and soft-spoken Cæsar Borgia possessed slender white hands, but his phenomenal strength was the fear of all. He was said to have cut off the head of a bull with one stroke of his sword.

We see then how great a factor in the flowering of the

91

Renaissance was the individual. The soil for a golden era of art was there; it remained only for the proper cultivators to plant the germ. History has shown us that the husbandmen of art have always been active, energetic, vital men.

To conclude, the Renaissance was not a miracle without cause or explanation. It was the result (1) of an innate love of life as well as culture in the Italian; (2) of the release from the solemnity imposed by primitive Christianity and the consequent liberation of the mind, body and spirit; (3) of the development of the individual by the hazards of his environment to an unparalleled degree of self-dependence, initiative and action. The opportunity element, too, while not of major importance, must not be overlooked. The release of men from military duties and warfare was a contributing factor in the widespread practice of the arts. And by no means least important is the encouragement of artists by wealthy princes and officers of the Church. Besides the economic aspect, the influence of these potentates in forming the tastes of the people was essential to the general cultivation and appreciation of painting.

The revival of pagan ideals was, as we said, patterned on the civilization of ancient Greece. First came sculpture which could most readily employ the pagan ideals of proportion and the beauty of the nude. Then came the period of research into the methods of painting. The discovery of perspective, the study of anatomy, of light and shade, interested painters a great deal more than the spiritual values of religion. Joy and beauty became the new religion.

*   *   *

MASSACCIO'S paintings, which carried forward the principles and ideals of Giotto, served as a standard and inspiration to young painters for many years. His influence was abetted by the sculptors, notably Donatello, who had turned to the classical models of ancient Greece and Rome. The art of painting became preoccupied with the representation of beautiful people, and from that it was only a step to preoccupation with the folds of rich draperies, the problems of perspective, the improvement of color, the representation of anything and everything as a display of the artist's virtuosity and skill.

For a time there was some danger of painting degenerating to mere exhibitionism, the easy admiration of the populace for the *tour de force* encouraging the artists in that direction. And the experiments of painters who wished to show how well they were able to reproduce with paint all the petty, involved accidents of nature, led to a sort of handmade photography on a grand scale. This was the first indication of what genre painting was to become in the hands of the later Venetians and the Flemish.

We reproduce a specimen of this kind of painting. It is the work of Ghirlandaio, in his day the principal painter of Florence. This picture, *The Adoration* (Fig. 19), is so overloaded with detail, that every square centimeter in the

93

canvas seems to be crawling with life. We have perfect perspective, a beautiful Madonna, a realistic Child, pedigreed live stock, ornamental architecture, horsemen, castles, floating angels and accessories. And yet the picture is devoid of spirit. We are not impressed. We take little interest in this teeming composition. It lacks the merit of simplicity and unity of statement which is so characteristic of the Primitives. The whole presentation is lacking in significance, the gestures of the figures in the foreground being especially commonplace. So that while the picture illustrates an incident, it does so only halfheartedly, without conviction. It is plain that the artist regarded his knowledge and ability as a painter sufficient in themselves. The result is excellent still-life painting; but movement, drama, significance, life itself, are absent. The lifeless product is only a step above mere decoration.

The same style of painting does not impose its restrictions so severely in the hands of an artist who is really motivated by feeling and conviction. We see in Filippino Lippi's *Apparition of the Virgin Before Saint Bernard* (Fig. 20) the same overcrowded composition employed by his teacher. There is no feeling of spaciousness in the canvas, no unity of line or rhythm, none of that harmony of design apparent in Fra Angelico's picture for instance. Each part of the canvas may be segregated and framed. But there is such dramatic significance in the presentation of the story, such conviction in the gestures and faces of the actors, that we

94

are made *to feel* the episode. It gets under our skin. It is great illustration.

Ghirlandaio's most illustrious pupil, however, was Botticelli. Whether we like his poetic conceptions and allegories or not, we must take cognizance of the fact that he brought to painting one of its most precious qualities, the rhythm of line. His is the most beautiful line in all European art. His rivals may be found among the Japanese but nowhere else. Without his innovations there would have been no Raphael, and even the art of Leonardo and Michelangelo owed much to him. But while these later and more famous painters used line only as a part of their general equipment, Botticelli's sense of harmonious rhythm escaped him at every turn, so that the result is, as Berenson says, "a symphony of line."

In Botticelli's *Spring* (Fig. 21), we see how graceful and flowing are the lines of the bodies and draperies. The very pose of the hands creates lines beautiful in themselves. The Florentine can be said to have founded the art of European line decoration. If the Englishman Hogarth had examined this picture of *Spring* instead of the back of a nude woman he would have found more *Lines of Beauty* than he could catalogue. The Victorian Beardsley, famous for his line decoration, only popularized the decorative quality of Botticelli's line.

But if his line has been more or less successfully imitated, few painters have achieved a rhythmic grace equal to his. We remember that rhythm is the repetition

95

of a kind of line. The sinuous, seductive harmony created by this repetition fascinates us in spite of the chaste character of his ladies.

In the accompanying illustration, for instance, the long line of the drapery of the center figure is repeated in the lines of the two figures to the left and in the lines made by the drapery of the young man and his lifted arm. The lifted upper arm follows the other upper arm. The long line of the young man's leg, from hip to foot, stops the leaning action of these diagonal lines. On the other side of the canvas, the group is held together by the arms, not only because the figures are holding on to each other, but because they follow each other in direction. The long curve made by the back of the young woman trying to escape the unwelcome embraces is repeated by the trees on the extreme right.

We cannot pass Botticelli without speaking of the types which he created. In his ideal of woman he is poetic, tender, a bit sentimental. There is an absence of sensuality, and in its place a dreamy lyricism. There is nothing profoundly religious, nor is there the materialistic spirit of some of his contemporaries. Instead there is the poetry of a sensitive, introspective person.

Botticelli's contemporaries who specialized in religious pictures were affected by his sentiment. Sentimentality in this swashbuckling day of the Renaissance was compelled to act as substitute for real faith. The Primitives knew little about painting but their faith was strong enough to express itself in spite of artistic limitations. But the spirit of early Christianity had so disappeared from Italian life that pictures for churches were more a decorative convention than a necessity. The story of the Bible continued to be the principal material for artists, mainly because churches were wealthy enough to compete with each other for talented men. The Popes were constantly on the lookout for newer and better painters. But artists approached their work cold and scientific, and where they sought to touch the sympathies of the spectator they did so by making their figures too expressive of dreamy emotion.

This is the criticism often made of Perugino. The first impression one receives from his pictures is that they are the work of a fervid religious mystic like Fra Angelico. But that Perugino was no kindly saint nor humble recluse is evidenced by the municipal court records at the time of his first visit to Florence, when he was arrested and fined ten gold florins for waylaying and beating a man. Historians call him an atheist and a villain. He was nevertheless a most accomplished artist and it matters little if his religious emotion was manufactured on demand. Mr. Leo Stein, in his book on esthetics, declares that emotion is unnecessary in the making of a work of art. He says:

One who looks at a picture will often have stronger emotions than the man who painted it; the spectators at a game will be more emotionally stirred than the players; the audience at the theater than the actors. . . . Most painters when they try to make a picture are perfectly cool.

97

If this statement which seems beyond dispute is accepted, one can have no quarrel with Perugino on the
ground of his being detached from his religious pictures.
It is possible that in his efforts to make us feel what he
himself does not, he overstresses the sentiment. But when
he is restrained, when he is at his best, as in his *Deposition
from the Cross* in the Pitti Palace and in his *Kneeling Christ*,
here reproduced (Fig. 22), neither Raphael, nor Leonardo,
nor Michelangelo is his superior. Besides his significant
manner of presenting his story and the uncommonplace
arrangement of his figures; besides his complete mastery
of form, of light and shade, of perspective, anatomy, line,
color, he introduces a new quality in painting, space, or
spatial relation.

In contrast to the crowded, teeming compositions of
Ghirlandaio and Lippi, and to the almost flat backgrounds
of Botticelli, Perugino gives us the illusion of different
planes and distances. There is a spatial relationship between
foreground and middle distance and distance which is just
as convincing as the more scientific experiments of Cezanne.
Giotto, by his method of presentation, could make us feel
sympathetic to his characters; Perugino, by his control of
space, by his convincing way of giving us the illusion of
vast, unlimited areas, plausible, peopled, built up, makes
us feel that we are a part of the picture. It is Mr. Berenson's
belief that the religious emotion so strongly conveyed to
us by Perugino is produced by this feeling of identification
with the universe—created by space-composition. There is

17. HEAD OF CHRIST—GIOTTO

18. FLIGHT INTO EGYPT — FRA ANGELICO

Courtesy Anderson, Rome

no doubt that the serenity which bathes his paintings is accomplished by his consideration of figures as masses placed in a given area, like the pillars of a building, or any other object. Such figures are architectonic, since they are handled as architectural masses.

To us Perugino remains the most typical Renaissance painter. Botticelli was somewhat withdrawn from the people; the princely Raphael, as we shall see, spent his short life exclusively in the company of popes and potentates; the scholarly Leonardo's mind was turned inward; Michelangelo brooded for a vanishing era. But this painter from Perugio who loved to crack a skull as well as his neighbor did, who practiced deceit and violence upon his fellows, was yet linked to them more closely than all his contemporaries, in art as well as in life. It is told that men, women and children ran to see his pictures; and that they came not of mere curiosity but because the calm and serenity of his compositions soothed them and made them forget the turbulence and violence of their existence. Scoundrel or not Perugino like no contemporary touched the hearts of his public. And if sentiment overlays his pictures it detracts nothing from their value as art.

7

LEONARDO, RAPHAEL, MICHELANGELO

➤➤➤➤◄◄◄◄

IF GIOTTO by his excellence and manifold achievements merits the name of genius, what title can we give to Leonardo da Vinci? In him are united all the intellectual and cultural attainments of the Florentines. In an age propitious to the muses few of his contemporaries rivaled him as poet, painter and musician. Princes besought his verses, convents his paintings. Add to these decorative accomplishments the man's many practical talents and he seems the most liberally endowed person in history. A

100

mechanical wizard, he invented countless appliances, telephone systems, musical instruments, machines; he was a designer of buildings, and a builder of waterways, sewerage systems, fortifications; and alone and untaught in natural science he was able to discover by observation, by attention to cause and effect, natural laws that paved the way for many modern inventions. It was he who first saw the possibilities of the aëroplane, and he who first discovered the principle of sound waves. His name is not unhonored nor unsung. But it is chiefly as the creator of a sweet, wistfully smiling lady called Mona Lisa that this prince of mortals is remembered.

It is not our intention here to demand more due for Leonardo's scientific accomplishments. We are concerned only with his painting. But we must be pardoned for looking askance at the famous Mona Lisa. It is our conviction that the master's less famous paintings are of greater moment, and certainly of more importance to our investigation. And so, avoiding comments upon his "soul," we shall seek his exact contributions to painting.

For a fairly long-lived man it is amazing that Leonardo left so few canvases. On the other hand when we consider the extent and variety of his activities we wonder that he found time to paint at all. The truth is that he was not essentially a painter. The job well done was not enough to give him satisfaction. To him paint was a means for exploring human and natural truths which eluded scientific apparatus and even words. The subtle, the mystical, the inexpressible challenged his command of the medium of paint. The things that he wished to say had never been touched upon by others. He sought new methods. He experimented with new colors, oils, materials of every sort. Through his anatomical studies he explored every problem of facial expression and gesture. The line between the poet and the scientist was lost. His notebooks are rich in comment and in odd drawings and sketches—a section of human skull, a part of a rare plant, the formations of clouds. This insatiable curiosity was reflected by a truthfulness in painting which had nothing in common with the realism of catalogued trifles.

Leonardo's paintings, however, were limited by this very quality of intellectual independence and curiosity. He could not complete a picture easily because he could not arrive at that complaisance which would permit him to leave it. The painted face or figure seldom equaled his conception; he changed and repainted constantly. The novelist Merejkowsky pictures him at work upon his fresco of *The Last Supper* over a period of sixteen years, painting when the mood came upon him, wiping out a face which he had finished the day before. His great undertaking for the Council Hall of Florence, begun in competition with Michelangelo, was abandoned as soon as the rough cartoon for the picture succeeded in expressing what he had intended to paint. Plainly he was not one of your Rubens type of artist who leapt from one canvas to the next in a frenzy to cover them and sign his name. His aim was

102

quality, but such is the irony of fate that the very urge for excellence which led him to experiment with new materials only succeeded in robbing the world of his masterpieces. His pigment has blackened, his surfaces crumbled away.

Certain valuable works, however, do remain. In the *Virgin Among the Rocks* (Fig. 23), in the Louvre, we have an opportunity of seeing an innovation of great importance: the use of landscape as an emotional factor. The mood of the canvas is created by the color, design and character of the background. To realize what a step forward this was we have only to recall the ineffectual paintings of Ghirlandaio in which the most dramatic incident is posed before a humdrum, stereotyped background. In creating a world sympathetic to his characters, Leonardo showed the same psychological insight which had led him to study minutely the vagaries of expression and meaningful pose.

Drama is the keynote in Da Vinci's work. In his efforts to produce an ever more powerful effect upon the beholder he exhausted all the methods of his predecessors. Significant grouping in Giotto's manner was not enough. Nor did individual gestures and strained faces satisfy him. The innovation above mentioned, that of fitting nature's moods to his subject, was a step towards fulfilment. However, it was his discovery of the dramatic importance of strong light and shade, chiaroscuro, to supplant the decorative line of the Florentines which most merits attention. A real pioneer in dramatic painting he pointed the ways which

103

were later taken by the two greatest dramatists with paint in history, El Greco and Rembrandt.

By no means the least of Leonardo's achievements was his ability to make of a portrait something more than a superficial likeness elegantly arrayed. The type was not enough; he must know the individual completely. Of course his unmatched knowledge of anatomy enabled him to express subtle traits of physiognomy with which his predecessors could only struggle. So we see that even the art of portraiture, generally regarded as a Venetian development, must pay its due to the great Florentine.

*   *   *

RAPHAEL'S exact contributions to painting are difficult to gauge. He was the most facile of Florentine painters and influenced by all of them. Regardless of the fact that he has remained for four hundred years the preëminent (popularly) artist of the Renaissance, he nevertheless marks the decline of its glory. He is essentially the people's artist, the illustrator. He is said to surpass by far his teacher, Perugino, but this heretofore universal opinion has lately been undergoing revision, and we are inclined to the judgment of the revisionists.

That Raphael invented types of beauty and pulchritude that have won the hearts of all classes of people in the civilized world is beyond question; but that does not seem to us the greatest accomplishment of the painter. In order

104

to achieve the soft, subtle modeling that will permit the dark eyes of his Madonnas to shine so warmly he is naturally compelled to sacrifice form. In fact his pictures lack form quite as much as Botticelli's without equaling the magic grace of the latter's line. In his less pretentious compositions and portraits, there is an apparent compromise between painting as practiced by Perugino, and the decorative line of Botticelli. It is a tribute to Raphael that he combined them so skillfully; in less able hands the two styles would be incompatible, incapable of fusion. In making these opposite methods into a style of his own the young genius apparently hit upon the elements of art most appealing to his fellow citizens.

Yet we shall see that he was capable of creative ability of a high order. His natural genius was for composition. In this field it is true he surpassed his teacher. Perugino had taught him the secrets of his art of attaining spatial relation. But Perugino himself regarded his figures, either singly or in groups, as masses placed in a given space. It is evident that he attempted to secure action and movement also; but in this he failed. In his picture we see numerous figures trying to run. But they are frozen in arrested action. The painter of masses could not handle his figures as intricate, decorative, mobile patterns; they are static, architectonic. Raphael was the first painter to compose a group from the point of view of *connected pattern*, so that his compositions are the most orderly possible, while still possessing movement. They are beautiful upside down or

105

in any postion, and they keep our gaze circulating about like the rhythms of Botticelli.

This use of pattern to secure movement is well illustrated in Raphael's fresco, *The School of Athens* (Fig. 24). Not only are the groups themselves inventively arranged, but the patterns of dark in the various figures "tie up" with each other to give the picture movement and unity. Nothing is isolated. In addition to this variety of pattern in the grouping there is a variety of pose and gesture in the individuals that recalls the dramatic stage setting of Giotto. The benefits derived from Leonardo's psychological studies in character portrayal and pose are also obvious. And while his figures do not possess the distinctive individuality that Leonardo's do, they are nevertheless gracious and fine in type and convincing in their expression. It is only when he is faced with the problem of painting portraits of ladies and Madonnas that he succumbs to popular demand and produces a too sweet, poorly modeled face. And in all his religious subjects he comes nowhere near the holy ardor of Fra Angelico for instance. His forte is never intensity of spirit, but rather a mastery of decorative, mobile composition, a richness of color, an undisturbed movement, and an ideal of beauty which has been the standard of the Western world for four centuries.

*   *   *

MICHELANGELO was a much stronger character. His personal force expends itself in his work. He does not aim to

19. THE ADORATION—GHIRLANDAIO

20. APPARITION OF THE VIRGIN—LIPPI

please, he is not a painter of or for the people, even though the people thrill to his work. He has ideals of beauty as well as Raphael. But while Raphael's beauty is of an effeminate, pure, adolescent, sentimental type, not visionary like Botticelli's, but real enough to be found in the flesh among the cultured, sheltered Florentines, Michelangelo's is an ideal that is almost Nietzschean—a lyrical, morbid, intense and brooding Superman. There is a fatalism, almost a despondency in the gestures and poses of his figures that reflect the state of his own being. There is a physical power that goes beyond the Greek or pagan worship of strength. Beauty in the sense of prettiness or grace is neither in his character nor in his work.

The man is gentle in heart but rough in manner. He is too melancholy to be the princely favorite that Raphael was. What causes underlay his somber spirit we can only guess. We do know that the wars, intrigues, and demands of his patrons kept him in a state of despair, bitterness, and fear. Seven of the best years of his life were spent on a selfish project of Pope Julius. This vain potentate commissioned him to erect a magnificent tomb for the papal remains. The project was never carried to completion. The years spent upon this futile, herculean task would have embittered sunnier natures. The realization that church and secular society were no longer motivated by considerations for the public welfare was enough to discourage him. He felt that the times were out of joint.

The days of the Renaissance were indeed coming to a

close. The followers of Raphael were enjoying great vogue. Totally without talent, they lent their imitative faculties to the manufacture of cheap, sentimental pictures which pandered to the moral decay. For attempting to restore Christianity to a fast disintegrating society the monk Savonarola is burnt at the stake. The pagan ideals of physical joyousness have degenerated into a flabbiness of self-indulgence. Art became the same thing that it is today among us—something to decorate the homes, to keep before our eyes images of pretty girls and flattering portraits done by avaricious craftsmen. The problems of form which thrilled Giotto's followers, of line which kept Florence spellbound in Botticelli's time, of space, which drew the populace of Perugio to see the canvases of Perugino, all these attainments in the art of painting now crystallized into nothing but a sugary sentimentalism. The old ideals of Florence were dying. And in the midst of this decay was Michelangelo, last of the titans, full of vigorous energy and poetic ideals. He felt himself cut off from his environment. His mind dwelled upon the glories of ancient Greece, upon the Superman, and these he painted. But he painted them in the disconsolate attitudes of hopeless mortals like himself.

His spirit alone might not have been sufficient to establish him as a great painter, however renowned he may have been as a sculptor. But he understood the demands of powerful painting as well as he did the carving of marble. Form to him was the essential of both. He strove for a

108

volume and bulk and weight just as Giotto had before him. He attained it in every muscle and anatomical form. He attained it by light and shade and by means of functional line.

By the latter method he was able to reveal the movement and direction of the form, just as an ellipse gives us the illusion of the roundness of the inside of a pail. Botticelli had made good use of functional line because it was his only way of expressing form; but his line was essentially decorative, beautiful more than functional. Leonardo, in his anatomical studies and in his sketches, showed how powerful line could be when used with the proper emphasis in the proper place, in the rendering of volume and round-ness. Michelangelo combined the two uses of line and for this reason he has been regarded the greatest draughtsman of the Renaissance.

With his death died the golden age of Florence. The religious spirit had given it birth, the pomp of the Church had sustained it. Now there was disintegration. Society fell apart. There was neither the spirit to guide it, nor the vitality necessary to the enjoyment of a carefree existence. The energy was spent, the body sick. The art of painting, like the art of living, moved northward in Italy to a more robust and pristine society, that of Venice.

8

THE RENAISSANCE IN VENICE

⫸⫸⫷⫷

W E HAVE devoted so much attention to the painting of Florence because the roots of all painting to greater or lesser degree may be traced to that illustrious city. Painters sprang up elsewhere who were more consummate craftsmen and technicians; but the theories and principles they employed were borrowed from such masters as Michelangelo and Leonardo. It is a curious fact that European art began by developing the theories of the *last* Florentines (realism, dramatic use of light and shade, etc.), and gradually

worked back to an imitation of the early mediæval Florentines such as Fra Angelico. Most modern painting, as will
be shown, is a complete denial of realism, striving instead
to capture the subjective. Not the sweet and sentimental,
but the realm of philosophy and poetic fantasy: ultimate
truth, not the surface.

If we jump blithely from Florentine painting to Modernism, however, we can carry little understanding to our
destination. As in the study of man, the evolutionary
process is important. (But unlike man, whose history is one
of constant outward refinement, painting *does not improve*
even superficially—it changes as the ideals of peoples
change. Criticism of a particular era of art is therefore
criticism of a particular people.) We shall see in Modernism vestiges of the methods of sixteenth, seventeenth
and eighteenth century painters. So to avoid confusion we
shall continue to follow painting somewhat chronologically.

Critics regard Venetian painting as the fulfilment of
Renaissance effort. The truth is that it is an entirely
different set of concepts. Whereas the principal characteristics of the Florentines are a lofty poetic sentiment,
an imaginative lyricism expressed in grace of line and
pattern, Venetian art reveals the preciousness of luxury to
extroverts and materialists. Art was not the preoccupation
of these Northern Italians. Their time was taken up rather
by business and conquest, with occasional feasts, pageants,
banquets, etc., for diversion. In Venice's heyday there was
little painting of importance. It was only after a series of

111

catastrophes overtook the State, reducing its potentates to figureheads and its merchant princes to retired gentlemen of leisure, that time and energy could be spared for the production of art. It was then that the need was felt for the preservation in painted documents of the vanished glory of the Republic and its leaders.

Instead of illustrating the Scriptures, then, the art of painting in Venice became an art of portraiture. The painters assigned to the tasks of representing important public men in their most sumptuous robes and in their most impressive manner bent their talents to these tasks. Whereas the Florentines painted drapery with the intention of revealing its beauty of line, or the sculptural form under it, the Venetians employed their skill in catching its texture, the sheen of its rich material. And where the Florentines painted a man or woman for the grace of his spirit, and the charm of hers, the Venetians wished to express the sitters' physical well-being, the fresh color of their complexions, the warm softness of the flesh. To them the painting of a beautiful nude was worth all the Martyrdoms of Saint Sebastians.

So we see that it is impossible to weigh the achievements of one school and those of the other on the same scale. Those of us who dwell in the world of the spirit will prefer the Florentines, the Primitives more than the accomplished masters such as Raphael; and those of us who find the illusion of soft, warm, scintillating flesh, and the representation of the glory of pomp and ceremony the greatest

112

achievements of the artist, will most certainly rate the Venetians superior.

In any case we must realize that it was Venetian painting, and not Florentine, which exerted the greatest influence over painting throughout the rest of Europe for the next three centuries.

*　　*　　*

WHEN Giovanni Bellini showed his talents as a portraitist the trend of Venetian painting was definitely established. Bellini abandoned the hardness and rigidity of Florentine painting. He practically eliminated line, depending entirely upon his color-values, his light and shade and his softness of change from one color to another, to obtain form. His figures are bathed in atmosphere and light. There is a tonal reality that has remained the aim of conventional portraiture to this day.

In his portraits the ideals of the Venetian portraitists are already evident. We see the rich texture of robes, the soft diffused lighting which obliterates outlines, the deep darks of the shadows, the individual character of the face, the dignity and well-being of the important personage. The background is simplified to a flat hanging, made interesting by the variations of light upon it. There is no involved, decorative view of a distant town, of rocks, of busy people—nothing to disturb the dignity of the subject. No Florentine except Leonardo visualized the possibilities of this kind of painting, and he was too far gone in the

113

traditions of his masters to do more than indicate them.

It is curious that Bellini should have as a pupil a poetic painter who in spirit was more a Florentine than a Venetian. Giorgione has much of the feeling of Botticelli, yet no two artists produced work more outwardly dissimilar. Bellini trained the young lyricist in the use of rich warm color, of light and atmosphere. Giorgione showed himself a faithful as well as an apt pupil. Not only was he able to put into practice the lessons of his master, but so much richer was he in qualities of heart and mind that he endowed his naturalism with a poetic conception unique among his contemporaries.

In his *Concert,* reproduced in Chapter 3, all the benefits of Bellini's training are evident. The heads are subtly painted, the character of each is definitely established, the atmosphere of the dark room is well conveyed. But in addition there is a composition of geometric pattern, a quiet orderliness and serenity reminiscent of Perugino, an expressiveness of pose which recalls Leonardo, and a feeling of human warmth or *gemütlichkeit* that reveals the gentleness of his own fine nature. He had many points in common with Raphael as well as with Botticelli. The gentleness expressed by each links them in spirit. Each left his mark upon the world in a short span of years, Giorgione dying at thirty-four, Raphael at the youthful age of twenty-seven. But their differences as artists are as sharp as the disparity in the ideals of their native republics. The Florentine, true to the traditions of his

114

21. SPRING—BOTTICELLI

22. KNEELING CHRIST—PERUGINO
Courtesy Anderson, Rome

culture, idealized his figures and faces in order to convey to us his poetic outlook, while the Venetian found in every person and type some human good worth recording. Giorgione's was perhaps the finer spirit, since it was more critical and less prolific. He left only a dozen paintings, whereas the brief span of Raphael's career is dotted with his prodigious work, much of which was in part accomplished by his retinue of helpers and students.

Giorgione's precepts did not completely dominate the art of Venice. The beauty of his paintings is not an obvious beauty; its appeal is naturally restricted to a cultured minority. Bidding for the approbation of the people was Carpaccio, a painter of a different stamp, trained by the brother of Giorgione's own master. This pupil of Gentile Bellini had acquired from the latter his primitive point of view. Carpaccio held fast to the crowded compositions teeming with life, the sharp outline, the minute detail, the architectural setting. To these he added his own naïve, humorous way of looking at life and its simple preoccupations. His pictures generally have dogs in the streets, birds in the trees, and all the homely little touches that appeal to ordinary people. This urge to tell in the plainest language the story of daily, ordinary life, revealing its charm as well as its meaninglessness, launched a new art in the history of painting—the art of *genre*. While Giorgione thrilled the cultured, Carpaccio delighted the multitude.

The tendency toward *genre* painting did not affect the

115

best painters. Giorgione remained their mentor and inspirer. His young friend Titian, like himself a pupil of Bellini, became his closest follower. Titian acquired from Giorgione all his technical skill and innovations and added to them his less serene, but lustier spirit. He was, after Leonardo, the first romanticist with paint. It is possible that he was influenced in his choice of subject, and even more in his dramatic manner of expression, by the many poets and writers who took refuge in Venice from the Inquisition in Spain. But whether it was this influence, the demands of his own nature, the incomplete experiments of Leonardo, or all three which acted upon him, it was he who carried Venetian painting to its destiny.

His exact contributions can be outlined. They were not so much the subtle qualities of the spirit which makes Giorgione difficult to explain. First he desired to express dramatic action. While Giotto accomplished this by a certain formal reserve, and Leonardo by a psychological understanding of types, and their habits, Raphael by grouping in fluid pattern, Titian sought to express the same thing by extravagance of gesture, which his knowledge of anatomy made interesting and convincing. To these means he added the striking atmospheric realism of Giorgione, attained by eliminating line entirely and diffusing the contours of his figures in the light which bathed them.

To add to the dramatic effect he improved upon Leonardo's use of landscape to reflect the mood of his subject. A somber subject such as the *Burial of Christ* was

116

aided in achieving its mood by somber sky and earth and trees in the background. A joyous, high-spirited event was supplied with joyous clouds and sunny earth as accompaniment.

This was a notable contribution to pictorial art, as we have seen. But it was not until the Venetians undertook realistic settings that the art of landscape painting was born. The observation of the artist was no longer confined to the human figure. The painter found it necessary to go outdoors to study the different aspects of nature, to sketch the accidental changes of color and tone. The romantic moods of sky and earth were found to be the surest support to a romantic composition. Only Leonardo had known this.

Titian is as famous for his innovations in regard to color as he is for his dramatic figures and romantic, atmospheric landscapes. The richness and warmth of his color were derived from Giorgione, but his work possesses nuances which his friend had never attained. The subtlety of refinement in his painting of flesh has been the inspiration to many other masters, notably Rubens, Watteau and Renoir. His ability to reveal the texture of rich materials went far beyond that of Bellini and of Giorgione. As a colorist he was the most accomplished painter of the Renaissance.

His nudes remain among the finest examples of the art of figure painting extant; the warm color, the fresh hue of the flesh, the subtlety of modeling, the natural grace of the pose, the sureness of the form, all are evident. The

117

reality which Titian has achieved in his nudes expresses fully the aims of Venetian art; this is especially clear when we see his women in contrast to the imaginative figures of Botticelli. Botticelli's nudes are symbols, of hope, charity, Spring, etc. Titian, on the other hand, was interested only in portraying a beautiful woman in a charming pose, and as real as possible, without making his picture literal or banal. The aspirations of the two Renaissance schools are best expressed by the nudes of these two painters.

The last of the great Venetians, and the one who combined all their attainments, as Raphael had those of the Florentines, was Tintoretto. Tintoretto's talent came to light at an early age and his father, unlike our more practical parents, did nothing to discourage him. On the contrary, he sent him to the atelier of the illustrious Titian. But the master was not long in recognizing budding genius of a rare order, and he did what was characteristic of his place and time—dismissed the prodigy from his class. This smallness of spirit seems incompatible with the attainments of the great painter, but having reached middle life, he could not bear to see himself decline in the esteem of his fellow citizens while a younger man, trained by him, supplanted him as the reigning painter.

Young Tintoretto did not bear his unkind master any malice. He continued to study Titian's pictures and search them for the secrets of their color. The motto on the wall of his studio read: *The color of Titian and the drawing of*

Michelangelo. He acquired some pieces of sculpture done in the classical manner and made drawings of them in various positions, placing them in the sharp glare of a lantern in order to secure dramatic light and shade. It was not only the outline, the contour, the functional line of Michelangelo which interested him, it was the volume of the planes, the modeling of the muscles and the form of the surfaces. To further his own instruction in drawing he made careful anatomical studies of corpses; to learn the secret of Titian's color he copied the master's paintings.

His energy did not stop at these ordinary means of acquiring knowledge. To him a canvas was a stage and the people upon it the actors. To attain the most dramatic arrangement of his figures, he modeled miniatures out of wax or clay, giving them the proper pose and gesture, and draping them with robes. He placed them on a stage constructed of wood and cardboard and moved them about until he achieved a satisfactory tableau. In this way he was prepared to reproduce the scene in paint with no doubts as to the effectiveness of the composition.

If genius is an infinite capacity for taking pains, Tintoretto deserves the appellation. Like most geniuses, however, he was slow in winning recognition. His personality disturbed the comfortable officials who had, like their brethren everywhere, an aversion to change. When he finally received commissions all his powers were put to the test. Tremendous compositions were demanded. His experiments in stage settings were not wasted; his mastery

119

of figure composition stood him in good stead. The study of perspective enabled him to handle vast crowded areas with conviction. The sharp light and shadow resulted in a new kind of composition of rhythms. Botticelli had achieved excellent composition by *rhythms of line*. Tintoretto created a bolder, more dynamic effect by *rhythms of light and dark*. The colossal scenes surpassed in their turbulence and vehemence anything attempted in the same spirit.

It is a matter of psychology whether this kind of turbulent, writhing presentation is more effective as drama than the restrained poetic feeling of the Florentines. Many of Michelangelo's figures are in the simplest poses, yet the easy movement of their torsos and legs and arms and the spirituality of the faces convey far more dramatic force than the excited figures. It seems to us that Tintoretto's drama was successful not by virtue of his rhetorical gesturing and excited poses but because of the strong light and dark which, in its rhythmic movement and sharp contrast, has the power to awaken our emotions. It is the dramatic effect of lightning flashing in a dark sky.

In his method of composition Tintoretto has many points in common with Raphael. The pattern of each is so arranged that the darks circulate through each group. Both artists have striven for variety of pose and gesture. But while the movement of Raphael's pictures is easy and well ordered, Tintoretto's is turbulent. The patterns are uncertain, the poses are rhetorical and exaggerated, the lights

120

strike against the darks sharply. Even the extravagant zigzag treatment of high lights and the use of an aura of light about dark figures and arms, serve to stress the drama of his scenes. This device is today one of the principal technical resources of Modernists.

With Tintoretto the aims and ideals of Bellini, Giorgione and Titian reached their end. The *genre* painting of Carpaccio found many followers; and Tintoretto's lessons in the technique of drawing and painting and composition became the equipment of artists who had little else than skill and aptitude for them. Veronese executed the most amazing feats in painting; but his pictures are devoid of spirit, whether poetic, religious, or dramatic. They are stupendous accomplishments, exhibitions of virtuosity. The virtuoso of the brush contributed nothing new to painting unless it was the casting off completely of classical traditions of costume, dressing his figures in the fashions of the day whether they belonged to his period or not. He was a naïve man who wished to express in pictures his joyous worldliness. It is interesting to note that his tremendous paintings of feasts were commissioned for the most part by religious orders and monasteries, which found great pleasure in riotous and lavish display. We see from this how far from the Christianity of the Primitives the Venetians had traveled at the sunset of the Renaissance.

9

EL GRECO AND RUBENS

꘎꘎꘎꘎

IF TITIAN is the truest representative of Venetian ideals in painting, he is also the arch-enemy, not of Modernists, who stand in awe of his achievements, but of Modernism, which finds his principles a reflection of a stupid, materialistic society living on life's surface. His talents were devoted to outward, surface beauty, free of implications and comment. Opposed to his sensuousness is the fervid spirit of Fra Angelico or the phantasmal "ultimate truth" of present-day Surrealists whom we shall later consider.

122

23. VIRGIN AMONG THE ROCKS—LEONARDO

24. THE SCHOOL OF ATHENS—RAPHAEL

Yet without Titian there would have been no Tintoretto. And without Tintoretto who was the first to employ rhythms of dark and light for dramatic purposes there might have been no El Greco. Who was this prophet El Greco, to whom all Modernists pay homage? He was, according to several eminent critics, the greatest painter of all time. But before telling of his accomplishments let us set the stage for his appearance.

First let us review the transition of Renaissance art. With the death of Florentine painting the greatest revival of Classicism since the pagan Romans can be said to have ended. We recall that Classicism in art means adherence to a system of proportion, the following of conventional, unrealistic standards. The Romans copied the Greeks, the Florentines copied the Romans. But with Leonardo's science and the Venetians' realistic temperament, Romanticism pushed aside the conventional. While Titian captivated the masses, Tintoretto set afire the ambitions of young painters by his unhesitating manner of picturing whole panoramas of Heaven and Hell just as if they had been posed for his benefit—nothing weird nor supernatural, everything lifelike and true to nature. Romanticism came to mean *realism in extravagant gesture or in turbulence.*

This doctrine of art captivated Europe. The Spanish temperament particularly was fascinated by it, adopted it, and remained loyal to it for four centuries. Every painter became a Romantic. But within the meaning of this term is such a latitude of difference in temperament and ideals, that the name can only be a pitfall to the novitiate in art. Men who from every scale of human values are found to be at opposite poles are indifferently called Romantics. Thus we have in the same breath, or in the same chapter, the names of Rubens and El Greco.

It is true that both are technically the heirs of Titian and Tintoretto. But as individuals they have nothing in common. Rubens is the Realist-Romantic, the painter of dramatic action as he imagined it in life; El Greco, on the other hand, is the painter of the realm of the spirit as he imagined it, and is a Romantic by nature of his dramatic force in depicting stories of the aspirations of man, the ecstatic, the unreal, the subjective.

When we said that the name of El Greco is apt to be in the same chapter in art books with that of Rubens, we were stretching the truth. The fact is that up to two decades ago the name of the expatriated Greek was scarcely men- tioned. As recently as ten years ago there appeared a compendium of painting in which a great chapter on Spanish Art failed to mention him even in the footnotes. A few American museums have recently obtained examples of his work, but the sudden rage of popularity that has swept over all civilized countries can only be attributed to the mystical inspiration his pictures hold for a world plunged ever deeper in materialism.

It was the French essayist and philosopher Maurice Barrès who in 1912 really discovered El Greco for the

124

world. Making a pilgrimage to the old Castilian city of Toledo he was able to see there, often in their original settings, dozens of masterpieces of the mystic. The impression created by these was so powerful that Barrès was moved to write a book explaining the reasons for the Greek's ecstatic art. He called this book *El Greco or The Secret of Toledo*. It was his thesis that the old city, huge clusters of Roman ruins, Gothic basilisks and Arab mosques, perched upon bleak, barren mountains and silhouetted against a blackish ripped-open sky, must inspire a religious terrorism in any painter's heart, particularly one with El Greco's background; and that only in its native settings can one grasp the significance of the man's work. This argument must only be tested to be found valid. Whoever has since gone to Toledo has come away thrilled. Hundreds of pilgrims journey annually to the little dingy church of Santa Tomé to stand enraptured before the *Burial of Count Orgaz*. Books on El Greco have appeared in all languages, their authors claiming that they and not Toledo possess the secret of the painter's art.

While the technical experts and the psychiatrists are holding the battlefield we shall advance certain observations which the reader can supplant at his leisure. A brief account of the facts of El Greco's life may be of use.

His real name was Domenico Theotocopuli. He was born in Candia in the Isle of Crete. The family migrated to Venice to the colony of Greeks who found living there profitable. The ornamental arts, particularly the making

125

of stained glass windows, were intrusted to Greek artisans whose Byzantine heritage fitted them for such work. It is possible that Domenico was the son of such an artisan. At any rate he is found at an early age an apprentice in the atelier of Titian. At this time Tintoretto and the Bassano brothers were enjoying sufficient popularity to attract to Venice the most ambitious young painters, so that however apt a pupil the young Greek may have been, there seemed little field in the tottering republic upon which he could win renown, or at least his daily bread.

He went on to Rome. The date of his arrival in the capital is fixed by the letter of a friend, Clovio, an old painter himself. This friend wrote in 1570 to the Cardinal Farnesa asking for work in behalf of his protégé. "A Cretan youth, Titian's pupil, has arrived in Rome ... his painting seems remarkable to me."

The Cardinal, it seems, held Clovio's judgment in high esteem, since he commissioned the young Greek to paint several pictures. These are now in the museums of Naples and of Parma, and elsewhere. They are distinctly Venetian in manner, recalling both Titian and Tintoretto.

Rome, however, was too overcrowded with painters to afford El Greco any opportunity to distinguish himself. About 1575, heeding the call of rich Spain, he set out for Castile. He found in Toledo an environment in accord with his nature. The town was the center of artistic life in Spain. Italian painters of the Roman school were at work on the Escorial, the magnificent palace of Philip II.

126

"El Greco must have eyed them (the painters) and their local brethren with disdain," says the biographer Cossio— and, we may add, with great envy and longing, since his hope was that the doors of the Escorial might be opened to him.

The first work which fell to him in Toledo was the commission for the altar-piece in the Church of Santo Domingo. This included five compositions and four single figures of saints. It was painted in 1577 and already marked a great technical advance over his Italian product.

A year later he painted his famous *Espolio* or *Christ Deprived of His Vestments*. This is one of the most dramatic of his compositions, but the reception which it met on the part of the Holy Fathers would have discouraged most men. He was asked to remove the nuns incorporated in the scene and the soldiers in armor standing about, as they were disrespectful to the figure of Christ. When he refused he was threatened with imprisonment. Fortunately both he and the picture escaped serious consequences. But that the painter was no prophet in his adopted country is easily apparent. A contemporary, Father Siguenza, speaking of Greco's *St. Maurice,* commissioned by Philip II, said, "It did not satisfy his Majesty and that is saying nothing, because it contented very few, although they say there is much art in it, and that its author knows much and that many excellent things have come from his hand." Such was El Greco's early reception by Spanish connoisseurs.

127

Nevertheless he was not discouraged. He continued to paint and to seek church commissions. And with the completion of his third great composition, *The Burial of Count Orgaz*, he established himself as the foremost painter of Spain. Convents and churches sought his services, and the élite Castilians bid for his talents as portraitist. About this time he began his mystical paintings which have remained the highest attainments of their kind in European art.

El Greco was a tireless, resourceful genius. Although not of the mental stature of Leonardo, his interests were almost as diverse. He was an architect, builder, sculptor, poet and writer. His pupils, notably a certain Pacheco, declared that their master was a great philosopher as well. His writings, however, are unaccountably missing. Yet we have only to glance at the inventory of books left by him at his death to see that he was a man of great intellectual appetite. There are twenty-seven Greek volumes, including Aristotle, Socrates, Plutarch, Homer, Euripides, Xenophon, Aesop, etc.; sixty-seven volumes of the most profound Renaissance Italian thought; a treatise on painting; nineteen volumes on architecture and seventeen miscellaneous works not described. These are in addition to the books written in Castilian.

The Spanish writer Tirso de Molino, a contemporary of El Greco, throws some light upon the painter's social life and his companions. Each evening the most gracious and cultured people of the city gathered to chat in the gardens of Buena Vista, across the River Tagus. "More was said in one word than in a book by a philosopher of Athens," says the writer. The great Cervantes, the playwright Lope de Vega, the eminent jurisconsult Covarrubias, the famous Cordovan priest Gongora were some of the painter's cronies. He upheld the Florentine tradition of Giotto and Leonardo and Raphael who by the magnetism of their speech charmed the most illustrious gatherings of their time.

El Greco's house in the old Jewish quarter had once been the elegant mansion of Samuel Levi, Treasurer of the King. The painter was extravagant in his ways. "He earned many ducats but spent them all in pompous living, and even kept paid musicians to play to him, that he might enjoy every pleasure while he ate," wrote his friend Martinez. From the inventory of his worldly goods, in which the furniture listed seems inadequate and even mean for the twenty-four fine rooms in the house, it is plain that elegance had given way to decay. And in the will there are more debts than dues; in fact, hardly any assets besides the two hundred unfinished pictures. From these facts we can reconstruct the picture of the man moving dignified and serene through life, oblivious to materialistic things, his mind ever wrestling with philosophical problems, and his desire for entertaining brilliant society the principal luxury indulged.

Now let us turn to his work.

El Greco's paintings can be divided into three groups:

Those which reflect his Venetian training, those which are chiefly technical accomplishments achieved in his first Toledan manner, like many of his portraits, and those which are expressive of his nervous, excitable, dramatic spirit. There were it is true times in his life as a portraitist when the face of a sitter would move him as much as a religious subject. At such times he strove to express character by means of distortion. No painter has used this device more successfully, possibly because with him it was an emotional urge and not an esthetic or technical principle. We shall see in our review of Modernists that some painters use distortion for purposes of design. Not so El Greco. When he distorted his figures it was to make them take on greater dramatic significance, to make us writhe in seeing them writhe. This, we remember, was the Byzantine method.

Dramatic force is obtained by another method. Tintoretto's sharp use of light and dark is employed much more effectively than the Venetian could foresee. The swirling lights and shadows instill in us the fear of the unknown and it is this quality of fear and religious ecstasy that grips us and reveals the inspired fanatic.

His color also serves his one purpose. He early abandoned the warm flesh tints of the Venetians. He discovered that he could obtain a heightened dramatic effect by painting most of his canvas in black and white color, giving pointed emphasis to his composition by adding a spot of vivid red or orange. He understood the psychological effect

130

25. CRUCIFIXION—EL GRECO

26. WINTER, OR THE HUNTERS—BREUGHEL

of color upon the spectator as no one had before him.
Since his belated discovery many Modernists have ventured
into the realm of the mystical and the supernatural. But
perhaps no mortal will ever approach him. The mystical
was in his Byzantine blood, the eerie drama in his Toledo
skies. Living three and a half centuries ago, this introspective Greek was the first Modernist.

The *Crucifixion* reproduced (Fig. 25) illustrates all his dramatic qualities. The pose and gesture of each figure are as
expressive as the arrested actions of dancers. In proportion
and drawing they are distorted, the figure on the extreme
right being enormously tall in comparison with the size of
his head. Even the angels are not immune from this treatment. The size of their hands is out of all proportion to
their forearms, especially in the one on the right. In the
Christ, the lower leg is much longer in proportion to the
thigh than is normal.

Just as effective emotionally as this expressiveness of
pose and gesture and exaggeration of drawing is the
rhythmic brilliance of light which moves excitedly from
one part of the canvas to another. Yet there is an organization or arrangement of figures and of lights and darks
which is the opposite of confusion. The lower figures are
almost symmetrical in their grouping, and the upper part
of the canvas is certainly so. We are not to infer from
this that all of El Greco's compositions are symmetrical.
But even in his most elaborate designs, where countless
figures writhe in ecstasy or despair, there is an organiza-

131

tion of mass and light and line which stimulates our emotions without confusing us or giving us the feeling of incompleteness. This is the secret of composition in painting.

Before leaving his picture, we may note that the emotional effect is also due to the use of the diagonal in his rhythms of light. To explain this statement we must digress a little. The painter can always depend upon an elementary device to convey the mood of his picture. This trick is the *direction of line* in a composition. For instance, when we wish to attain a mood of quiet, rest, the opposite of activity, we make as many lines as possible horizontal. The seascape, the prairie, the deserted street, suggest this means. Again, when we wish to convey the religious mood, awe, reverence, we use as many vertical lines as possible. We soar to Heaven. This is the principle employed in Gothic architecture. Tall trees in the forest affect us much the same way. The feeling of peace and plenty, contentment, the abundance of nature, is expressed by curves. Rolling hills, sheep, fruits and vegetables symbolize abundance and are expressed in round lines. But the emotion opposed to all of these, the dramatic emotion, is expressed by the diagonal. Slanting rain, lightning, the brandishing of sticks, the lunge into action, are all so conveyed.

Looking then at El Greco's composition with half-closed eyes, we see that the two angels in the upper section of the canvas slant to the right. This action is accomplished by the use of light rather than by line. The diagonal is

132

repeated in the lower group most forcefully. We can follow the arm of the kneeling girl to the point where it joins the sharp light of the fold in the disciple's gown. Both light and dark emphasize the diagonal.

So much for El Greco's technical means of attaining drama. While analysis may clarify his composition and turn apparent confusion to dramatic power, no picking of a canvas to pieces can uncover the sources of the painter's ecstatic Orientalism. There is a school of critics who maintain that he was the victim of insanity. But their hypothesis is unfounded in view of the painter's most rational and brilliant command of organization. Others have attributed his peculiar methods to the consuming egotism of the man, who feared to be accused of painting like Titian, and so sought to be wildly eccentric. This is a negative argument since it fails to account for his superior powers. The latest interpretation of El Greco's transformation from an ordinary Venetian painter to the Toledo mystic is from the pen of a Spaniard, José Merediz. This critic states with tiring redundancy that the young Greek was so struck with the beauty of the stained glass windows in the Toledo Cathedral that the urge to translate their spiritual force into paint possessed him and also lent him the technique with which to do it. This explanation is far-fetched.

To understand the nature of the work, we must keep in mind the facts pertaining to the man. He was born in a Greek city with a Byzantine tradition. He was then an

133

Oriental. He came fresh from jovial sunny Italy to a city which not only by its physical Arab character and frightening setting was enough to awaken his imagination, but which was submerged in an Oriental ritual that must have spoken to him in loud and familiar voices. We must keep in mind that Toledo, while a stronghold of Roman Catholicism, was peopled by a race of Spaniards in whom were fused the Jew and the Arab. So that not only in the architecture of the city, but in the song of the people, in their nervous reactions and mental qualities there was everything to appeal to the atavism of El Greco and evoke responses from him as Italy never could do. His is the spirit of Fra Angelico and of the Hebrew prophets; of Chassidic songs and the tortures of Arab devil dancers. The lucid mind is driven by aspiring heart to put down in paint what remains today a shrine for the troubled, drifting Westerner.

*　　*　　*

WHEN El Greco died, the Flemish painter Rubens was at the height of his career. Like the Spanish Greek he was noted for his social grace. Not even Leonardo was more at home in the company of kings and princes. In the capacity of diplomat he passed from one palace to another settling affairs of state and painting compositions and portraits in his leisure. At an early age he was invited to the household of the Lord of Mantua, Gonzaga, and so had many opportunities to study the work of the Venetians.

134

Their influence is apparent in all his paintings. He was an ardent admirer of Titian's color, particularly in the latter's paintings of nudes; he was evidently greatly impressed by Titian's *Bacchus and Ariadne*, a swirling dynamic picture of pagan pleasure. There is no doubt that Rubens felt himself atune to the note of animal joyousness struck occasionally by Titian.

The Flemish painter's compositions are often as involved as Tintoretto's; his figures gesture as violently. For this reason he is called a Romantic. There is a total absence of the romantic spirit in his work for all his borrowing of romantic traps. His faces are pretty but often banal. His drawing is sometimes crude, his compositions uninventive and tiring, his carelessness in rendering form often apparent; but while these limitations may be dismissed, his point of view is subject to endless debate and criticism.

For whether he is painting crucifixions, nudes, or scenes of violence, he is seldom more than a realist. His Christs have nothing of the spirituality of the Christs of Perugino, of El Greco, of Giotto. They seem rather to have been posed for by the village blacksmith. His nudes are not the ideally beautiful women of Titian but are more often the girls whose voluptuous amplitude prompted him to engage them as models. His nudes are therefore nothing more than portraits of exuberant types pleasing to his fancy. They are not esthetically ideal. We shall see in our survey of Modernism that the present-day artist also dispenses with

135

types which conform to the tastes of the spectator. But the difference between an enormous nude with bulging fat as painted by Picasso and as painted by Rubens is of fundamental importance. In the hands of the latter it is the woman who appeals to the artist; while the Modernist is intent upon the swelling volume and form and the rhythm of line for *their own sake,* thus creating a new and harmonious ideal.

Putting aside matters of ideals, we must attribute to Rubens the development of the art of color. With the passing of the Venetians he was the only great colorist left in Europe. He carried his experiments far beyond the range of Titian. He found nuances in the painting of flesh that had never before been apparent; so that there is hardly a square inch in his acres of nudes which is not beautiful in color. His own lusty, assertive nature establishes him as a personality embodying not only the ideals of his race, but of all painters of all time and place who are mentally and biologically constituted like him.

The influence of Rubens in the development of painting is historically of the greatest importance. A corps of students executed his involved conceptions: among them Jordaens, whose rather ordinary mind was able to add little to his master's art, and Van Dyck who far surpassed his energetic teacher in grace, feeling and technical skill.

But the lessons of the Flemish master were not confined to his studio. They were spread to foreign countries by his visits on affairs of state. In England it was his paintings rather than his diplomatic genius which caused him to be knighted. Marie de Medici brought him to France to make the colossal decorations which are now in the Louvre. Philip IV of Spain who first received him coldly, since he had little confidence in diplomats who were artists, was very quickly charmed by his person and his painting. The mollified king even gave him a studio in his palace, and here Rubens made the acquaintance of the young court painter, Velasquez. It is fairly evident from a perusal of the Spaniard's work that the dazzling realism of the Flemish courtier-artist captivated his responsive pupil. No painter's influence had ever been more widespread.

10

THE PORTRAITISTS

→»→»«←«←

AT THIS point we are at the crossroads of the art of painting. In one direction points El Greco, the philosopher mystic, in another the flesh and blood hand of Rubens indicates the way. If we must remain silent when asked "What is art?" we can at least see clearly the two sharply opposed aims of these leaders. For centuries Europe followed the path of Rubens, the sensuous, materialistic, consummate craftsman. In Modernism the path chosen was El Greco's.

138

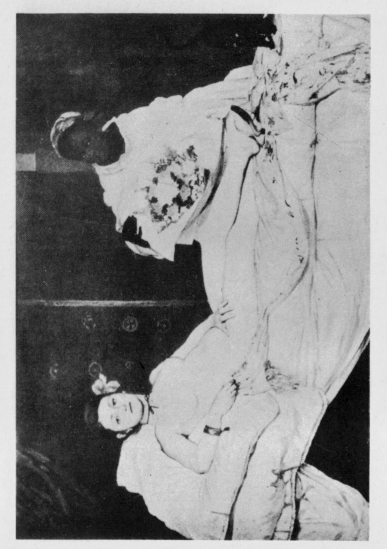

27. OLYMPIA—MANET

28. THE STAIRCASE—MONET
Courtesy Durand-Ruel

All portraiture is of course in the tradition of Venice and of Rubens. The earthly need for a record of an individual's appearance, whether for love, reverence, memory of the dead, or merely to satisfy the vanity of the sitter, established the portrait as a vital part of life in a cameraless day. You had to train yourself to catch the likeness and give the sitter dignity. If you could add nice color and clever brushwork so much the better. The problem was simple and clear. The portrait was an instrument of social service.

The mystic picture is conceived differently. It springs from no other need than the urge of the painter to express himself. It is demanded from within not imposed from without. It need not have fine color or clever brushwork since these qualities can only titillate while often detracting from the singleness of the message. Technic is not important. Finally the mystic picture is an instrument for the individual in achieving some spiritual truth and is not intended to delight masses. For this reason its worth is indeterminate and varies for each spectator.

For three hundred years painting had been the art of Portraiture. To-day, among Modernists, it is a quest for higher truth, a mystic exploration.

The complete disintegration of pre-modern painting is visible in the fashionable portrait of the present. All truth and candor are ditched. The artist fearfully flatters his customer, anxious to avoid court actions and eager to find his next commission. Cleverness of brushwork is made the important element in judging the canvas. Yet it is possible for portraiture to embody qualities of mind and spirit. We recall that one of Leonardo's principal traits was his interest in expressing the inner character of his sitter. The Venetians substituted nobility and dignity for character. Rubens replaced these by attention to ruddy color and by investing his creatures with a certain lustiness. Van Dyck, more clever than his master, restored elegance, specialized in elegance, made elegance the end of art and art the possession of the elegant. Franz Hals painted boisterous commoners in a dumb-show of mirth, but the shorthand cleverness of his brush has proven even more captivating to society painters than the refined splendor of Van Dyck. The lessons of Leonardo were ignored.

That is, until the advent of the one painter who found in the faces of humble humanity the same satisfying qualities of poetic mysticism which El Greco found in distorted phantasmal compositions. That painter was Rembrandt. Rembrandt began his career as a society portraitist.

In his early years he was simple enough to paint his patrons in a conventional manner; but with maturity and the development of his faculties he felt the urge for more personal utterance. He dared to express that superfluous and unwelcome thing, the truth. The result was an old age of poverty, accompanied by the production of some of the most esthetically thrilling canvases the world has to offer.

140

Rembrandt's honesty is not the honesty of Rubens who chose to paint fat young women because he liked fat young women. It is the honesty of a poet whose discoveries of beauty in the commonplace prompt him to express them for the delectation of ordinary mortals (who more often than otherwise, do not wish to look at them).

He found more poetry, and more character, in the faces of the lowly, hardworking poor, than in those of the well-to-do, contented bourgeois. Our reactions to his canvases are mixed with speculation: We wonder what the life of the seamy-faced person emerging from the picture before us must have been. In this respect the painting approaches illustration. Nevertheless the picture is lifted above illustration into the realm of painting at its best by painting, and not literary, qualities.

Whether his work was the result of his interest in the researches of Leonardo, whether it was due to the influence of obscure compatriots, or whether it was the personal development of a painter whose sight was defective, is a question not yet determined. He was known to have been a collector of the works of the great Italians, and although his own approach has little in common with the Florentines he admired, it is quite possible that the experiments of Leonardo in securing dramatic delineation of character by means of strong light and shade impressed him. He was almost entirely self-taught, so that the influence of the colorists descended from Rubens had little opportunity to reach him. And it is also possible that he was so optically impaired that he saw only the most salient surfaces of things emerging into the light from mists and shadow. Myopia may have helped to make the master.

Whatever the cause, his painting embodies the most sensitive and yet most dramatic use of chiaroscuro in the history of portraiture. Design or pattern as employed by the Florentines has no place in his canvases. Nothing matters but the form of the surface or object as it is seen to come forth from its background of indeterminate atmosphere. Form and *significance*. The unimportant details are ignored. The local color (or color proper to each object), used by the Florentines to create a design, in his work is subordinated to the warm yellowish tone which envelops the whole canvas. Unity, completeness, dramatic effect, are attained by tone, an envelope of atmosphere, instead of by color and line. There is no formal composition, no definite outline, no classical point of view, no pretension to elegance which is not elegance of the spirit.

While Rembrandt lived in wretched obscurity, painting his own portrait time after time for want of any other model, the favorite of the Spanish court was pleasantly engaged in painting the royal household. Velasquez has been termed by many critics the greatest painter of all time, but the honor has also been conferred upon Raphael, and there is no one to act as arbiter. Like Raphael, Velasquez was an eclectic, that is, he profited by putting to use what went before him, rather than developing, as Rembrandt did, an individuality based upon his limitations as well as upon his independent observation of nature. The Spaniard apparently had no limitations.

Because his hand never faltered, because nowhere in his many canvases is there evidence of perplexity, experiment, change, Velazquez is considered the king of all figure painters, the consummator of all the worthwhile in European art. This is unquestionably true if we regard European art as a technical progression struggling to conquer matter. Velasquez followed the guiding hand of Rubens and reached the end of the trail. Rembrandt did not follow the road taken by the other portraitists but blundered into the camp of the mystics. He is perhaps the only portraitist who so lost his way.

11

LANDSCAPE AND GENRE

❯❯❯ ❯❯❯ ❮❮❮ ❮❮❮

WHILE PAINTING had been established throughout the rest of Europe as an art of and for the well-to-do, the artists of the Netherlands were content to find their subject matter in the lives of simple burghers and even less respected society. Rembrandt, then, was not alone in his predilection for the lower stratas. Yet he was hardly more the people's artist than Rubens and Van Dyck since his somber nature segregated him from a naturally light-hearted, genial people.

144

The true art of the Netherlands was the art of genre. Genre literally means kind or type. A picture which has for its subject not individuals, but a whole class of society or a particular type of setting is a genre picture.

Dutch and Flemish genre differ from the detailed cataloguing of Ghirlandaio's backgrounds and even Carpaccio's photographic assemblies. The interior of the home, intimate society, the moods of nature, are here invested with, and held together by, a pleasurable sentiment. Over all there is a sense of the friendliness of nature to man, of man's being at home in the world.

The art embodying these qualities was practiced long before the great figure painters came upon the scene, and long after they departed. If Rubens completely overshadowed his little contemporaries, they in turn were affected only technically by his achievements. They gave pleasure to their neighbors by painting pictures of the simple life. Today we are discovering these records of the times and of the diversions of the people. The manner in which they are depicted charms us more than the virtuosity of the prodigious and energetic Rubens.

Genre was the expression of a society in which the family was the all-important unit. As an art form it can have no great vogue today for instance when mankind is sophisticated, or industrialized, or intently burrowing for individual aggrandizement. The keynote of Dutch genre is a joyous warm humanism. If this is a quality foreign to

145

us in actual life, it is still occasionally achieved *in pictures* by a few Modernists.

Three attributes of modern painting are traceable to the work of genre artists. First, the objective attitude towards the commonplace subject; second, the odd use of color; third, the naïve good humor. We shall see that it was an easy progression from the lowly scenes of farmyard and interior to the romantic peasant of Millet (even though he appeared two centuries later), and from the latter's rustic scenes to the astounding objectivity of Van Gogh, a Modernist inheriting the Dutch tradition. As regards the use of color two methods are apparent. One is the sharp pattern of related colors similar to the Florentine method (but more subdued and neutral in quality); the other is the strong use of light concentrated in a few spots. Neither of these methods owed anything to the realism of Rubens. Today we find both usages in modern painting. In the picture by Breughel, painted about 1565, the warm, earthen color is as distinctive as the conception. Its unusual relationships have obviously impressed such prominent Modernists as Utrillo and Chirico. As for the naïveté and good humor (qualities with which the Breughel overflows) a whole school of Modernists (with the unwitting Rousseau at its head) has steadfastly maintained the tradition.

Breughel's picture of *Winter, or the Hunters* (Fig. 26), as it is officially called, is a minute, almost literal rendering of landscape and people. His trees, birds, housetops, people, and particularly his dogs, have the quality of decorative

146

29. TAHITIEN—GAUGUIN

30. MAN WITH RED HAIR—VAN GOGH

silhouettes, such as we see occasionally cut in sheet metal. (Rousseau also employs this kind of pattern.) And not only are these near-silhouettes beautiful in themselves, but in the grouping and general organization of the canvas such perfect order is achieved, that our eyes move over it in definite, easy steps, from one pattern of dark to the next.

Another painter of genre, only recently rescued from two hundred years of obscurity, is Vermeer of Delft. His pictures, while as objective as those of Velasquez, are almost lyrical in their handling. He painted furniture, and walls, and figures in silk, with the same feeling that Giorgione, and later Corot, experienced in painting landscape. To him the problems of light and atmosphere in a room were as important as the light and atmosphere of woodland and meadow, and as romantic as a sunset. (Van Gogh's approach to his subject, while less restrained, was essentially the same.)

It is surprising to find Vermeer's work so similar in spirit and in actual painting to the work of Giorgione. We find the same rigid, classical, geometrical patterns; the same serenity, the same kindliness, pervade the canvases of each. Only in technical grasp does Vermeer surpass the Venetian. His color is more original, more subtle in its nuances, and his ability to reproduce the soft flood of light as it enters a room shows how far beyond the Italians the painters of the North went in matching the appearance of nature. The work of Vermeer, therefore, has the distinction of embodying the superior realism (or Romanticism) of

147

the Dutch genre painters while remaining classical in approach and in feeling. In its use of geometrical design and form it rivals the Italians.

Classicism and Romanticism—we pause here to consider the origins of the two major political parties of painting from the Renaissance to the virtual dissolution of the art with the advent of Impressionism. These camps were as sharply divided as Slave Holders and Abolitionists. Without their periodic attacks upon each other it is doubtful if European academic art, an aging parent between two brawling children, would have marshaled the energy to drag out its existence as long as it did. Yet these sallies, sorties, thrusts and counter-attacks effectually clarified the aims of painting in such a way that Impressionism and the subsequent movements were inevitable. For this reason it is well to review the war. It is important to note that the leaders of the opposing factions were not figure painters but landscapists.

The Frenchman, Claude Lorraine, was the first official Classicist after the Renaissance. He borrowed Italian architectural settings and other conventional accessories and combined them in a kind of unreal landscape which became a standard for all Classicists. He was not, however, the first landscapist. As early as Perugino we have the art of landscape conceived, not as mere drawing or decoration, but as air and space. The Venetians, too, in following Leonardo's discovery of the moods of nature, produced many fine backgrounds, atmospheric, and based upon care-

148

ful observation. Titian made a number of sketches out-of-doors. The poetic Giorgione composed pictures in which the figures were hardly of greater importance than the scenery in which they appeared. And in El Greco's view of Toledo we have a modern landscape whose fidelity to the actual scene is overshadowed only by the dramatic presentation of the artist. Rembrandt was a contemporary of Claude, and that he too was drawn by the art of landscape is apparent from his famous painting *The Old Mill*. But for some unstated reason historians begin their accounts with the work of the two chieftains of the rival factions, Claude, who lived in the time of Rubens and Velasquez, and the Dutchman, Ruysdael, who was born more than two decades after his rival, but who died in the same year, 1681.

The difference between the two painters is the difference between the Latin temperament with its roots in the formal and classical art of antiquity, and the romantic, or realistic, or sentimental traits of the Flemish and Dutch mind. This difference is readily apparent in their work. That of Claude seems as artificial as a stage setting. Yet the grasp of the problems of light, perspective, composition and spatial feeling overcome the artificiality which strikes us at first glance. It is nature, yet it is an unfamiliar, legendary world.

Ruysdael, on the other hand, gives us not the elements of painting as much as the elements of nature. He touches us by his paintings of romantic but real things. He catches nature's melancholy moods and we react sympathetically to them because we are able to identify them. The fleeting accidents of light which two hundred years later intrigued the French Impressionists, are the chief problems of the Dutchman. While Claude sets down in majestic pomp the eternal, unchanging aspects of his scene, Ruysdael captures the one moment in nature which would make us stop and exclaim, "Ah!"

His dramatic or romantic or realistic spirit, or whatever it may be called, was superior to his technical means however. The art of figure painting, perhaps because it was more remunerative, perhaps because it was older, had advanced far beyond landscape in its mastery of the problems of color and light. Rembrandt, working almost in monotone, derived his effects by the subtlety of his tones; the yellowish brown of his interiors was transferred to his paintings of the outdoors. This tradition of painting trees and grass brown held Ruysdael in its grip. It remained for the English landscapists to discover the actualities of color in nature.

Gainsborough was the foremost of the early painters to feel the spell of Dutch landscape. In his own numerous studies from nature, however, he added little to the accomplishments of Ruysdael. His rôle was to make known the Dutch painter's methods and so affect the development of the art in England. The racial similarities in temperament between the Dutch and the English made the cultivation of the ideals of Ruysdael a much more natural pursuit

150

than the importation of the formal precepts of Claude. Realism seems to the English mind a prime essential of art and Gainsborough served his country by introducing the realistic landscape. It remained for Constable to take the step forward necessary to the growth of the art. What he accomplished was the introduction of color instead of shades of brown. He painted grass somewhat green instead of the conventional color, and in addition he secured an effect of light and atmosphere which was shocking to all the painters of the old school. In the closing years of his life, he saw his art responsible for the existence of one of the most important groups of landscape painters in the history of art, *i.e.*, the Barbizon School.

Before going on to them, however, we must give some attention to the art of Turner. The English critic, Ruskin, has pronounced him the genius of Western civilization, .or at any rate, the foremost artist in England, which to him meant the same thing. What Turner actually accomplished as a painter is little in comparison to the direction he pointed out for the development of landscape art. In his oils he stuck to the formal classical ideals of Claude Lorraine, not because he felt sympathetic to Latin classicism but because the unreality of artificial arrangement permitted him to indulge his penchant for idealistic scenes, too theatrical to have any basis in nature. It was, however, in his use of watercolor, which afforded his genius for extravagant color nuances full play without the restrictions imposed by the observance of formal art, that he showed

151

what the possibilities of landscape really were. The brilliance of these watercolors, their abstract, decorative beauty, did as much for the development of painting into French Impressionism as Constable's work had done for the French Romantics of the Barbizon Forest. It is curious to note that these two Englishmen were largely responsible for the two schools of landscape which made France the art center of the world in the nineteenth century.

12

THE FRENCH TRADITION

➤➤➤➤◄◄◄◄

SINCE IT was France that drew the eyes of the world
to its painters in the last century, let us see where the
origins of its national art lay. After the decline of Venetian
art Rome had become the center of Italian painting, not
because there flourished in the capital city great masters to
whom anxious students made their pilgrimage, but because
it was rich in collections of masterpieces. It was the last
stronghold in Italy of the classical traditions which were
being displaced by a sensual materialism on the one hand,

and by an enervated false sentimentality on the other. But Rome was overcrowded with painters, as we have seen from the exodus of El Greco.

Nevertheless the ambitious art students of all Europe turned their footsteps to the Eternal City. Among others was a sickly, poverty-stricken youth by the name of Poussin. Poussin had left his little hamlet in the north of France and after many discouraging vicissitudes, had made his way into Italy. He wanted to be a painter in the classical manner; his ambition was not just to paint what he saw, but to set down the stories and legends of antiquity. In Rome he found an environment that encouraged his penchant for the glories of the past. He transferred to his canvases the antique sculpture in which the city abounded; his figures pose lifelessly in splendiferous, imaginary settings. And in addition to borrowing the subject, the pose, the proportions and even the spirit of a distant epoch, he studied well the compositions of the Florentines and the technical methods of the Venetians. He did not succeed in breathing much life into his creations, but he was, together with his exiled compatriot, Claude, responsible for the foundation of a taste in painting which opposed the tendencies of the North. And in addition, he gave an impetus to the art of painting in France that brought about its sudden rapid development. If he added nothing that was precisely new, he at least succeeded in stating with paint the ideals of a great number of his less talented contemporaries.

154

31. THE CIRCUS—SEURAT

32. SEATED LADY—MATISSE

From his precepts there grew a body of practitioners who were so pleased with their own interpretations of Classicism that they formed an exclusive little society, the French Academy. Their aim apparently was to guard the art of painting against any assault upon its classical intentions. Under the presidency of Le Brun they did prodigious work towards this end by ignoring all painting except their own. If Poussin added little to the art, they added less. They are chiefly important for having opposed the genius of the period, Watteau, and for having voted against him when he competed for the Grand Prix.

Watteau, like Raphael and Giorgione, failed to reach the prime of life. He died at the age of thirty-five. But unlike his illustrious forerunners, his curtailed existence is not a record of gentleness and serenity of soul. He was a stormy, impetuous character who seemed to have divided his time between painting quietly romantic pictures and making enemies of his benefactors and friends. His difficulties with pedantic teachers may have been due to his temperament, but the fact that the precepts of the Classicists were officially and implicitly accepted as fundamental to art in France was no little factor in the conflict between him and other artists.

He was by every natural cause a Romantic. Though born in France in the little town of Valenciennes he was of Flemish ancestry. From this fact we see that the rigidity of the Classicists was antipathetic to his northern nature. And the early opposition of his father, the town plumber,

to an art career compelled the boy to learn to draw by
sketching people in the street, that is, by *observation* instead of by an infallible system. Even when his father re-
lented and sent him to study with an obscure painter in the
village, it was from the canvases of Rubens' followers,
Teniers and the genre painters, that young Watteau absorbed his ideas of color, composition and technique. The
tenets and methods of the lowland painters found responses
in his own nature. If Vermeer was a classicist in a romantic country Watteau was the very opposite.

The urge to paint things and people in his own way was
hampered by a hostile environment. At the age of eighteen
he ran away from home, arriving in Paris penniless. He
found employment in the service of a decorator, and this
fact too sheds some light upon his mannerisms, particularly
the stylized elegance of pose and arrangement. Later he
found more congenial work making decorations for the
Grand Opera. The life of the theater absorbed him. The
artificial pageantry, the rhetorical affectation, the elegance
of manner, the queer people who loll about and sway and
curtsy, all found a place in his pictures. But his artificial
world was not an offensive one. It was peopled with figures
a little fantastic, charming nevertheless. And the restrained
manner of the artist saves him from any criticism with
regard to matters of taste. Always he is genteel. This is not
to say that he was mild or effeminate. Above everything
else, his pictures possess a vitality completely absent in

the work of the Classicists whose formal, lifeless figures stand like frozen images in arrested action.

Much of Watteau's vitality is the result of his early sketches of his townsmen. In his drawings of street types he achieved a piquancy and an originality which establish him as the oustanding draughtsman of the eighteenth century. And in his technical grasp upon the problems of paint he is much stronger than his contemporaries. He employed the warm tones of the Venetians and set them off with silvery nuances. Rubens' cool reflections evidently suggested to him the effects to be attained by playing the silvery tones against the deep warm notes of the Italians.

However immeasurably advanced over his contemporaries was Watteau in painting ability, it is in the realm of fancy that much of his significance lies. The human warmth of which we spoke permeates his paintings and is transferred to us with magic ease. If Watteau inspired Cezanne centuries after him to bring the method of contrasting color to a culmination, his vague, half sentimental, unworldly romanticism will continue to distil its subtle charm when theories of color will have been exhausted.

The effect of Watteau's paintings was to break down the influence and the dignity of the Classicists. But little good came of this rebellion. The painting practiced in his name did nothing to raise the standards of French art. The Louvre galleries in Paris have many examples of the work of his followers, notably of Boucher and Greuze. These painters appropriated the technical accomplishments of their prede-

157

cessor and something of his preference for the fanciful world. But they fall so far below him in spirit, conception, significance and every other quality not precisely that of craft, that instead of supporting his principles, they serve only to reflect the general spiritual decadence of the times. Greuze slyly preaches morals in an age that has no use for them except academically, and he is careful to select for his holy lessons the most voluptuous models. Boucher invades the Eden of nudes floating on clouds accompanied by angels and cupids. Neither painter understands the important contribution made to the art by Watteau's discovery of the use of warm and cool color.

The painter Fragonard came nearest to the ideals of the master, but only after the movement away from formal Classicism had died of anæmia. The end of the eighteenth century was already too far from Watteau's ascendency for the revival of an art which had suffered so much in the hands of small-spirited men. The star of Classicism began its rise once more, this time under the guidance of David. David went back to the legends of Greece and Rome and painted great compositions of many figures which by comparison made the static creatures of Poussin appear as animated as dancers. He not only contrived to have his posing people suspend all motion, but in his use of cold color he attained the deathly stillness of a marble world. The livid hues of his faces even hint of petrifaction.

But such was the influence of David that at the beginning of the nineteenth century he stood in complete control of

33. NICE – DUFY
Courtesy Valentine Gallery

34. BAPTISM OF CHRIST—ROUAULT

French art. Every ambitious student found his way to the
studio of this scholar of antique lore. Discussions on
theories of art resolved themselves into questions of Greek
history and social custom, rather than into problems of
color, form, design. But with the entry into David's fold of
rebellious and independent spirits the discussions returned
to the old argument of Classicism versus Romanticism.
The youthful painter Gericault, before he died at the age
of thirty-four, split the ranks of David's pupils by his
compositions of writhing figures done in the manner of
Tintoretto. His *Raft of the Medusa,* a tremendous canvas
depicting a shipwrecked group of half-dead survivors,
shocked all Paris with the tragic realism of that event. But
for the most part the picture was viewed by critics as a
brutal denial of art, and stared at as a curiosity.

There was no body of criticism to take up a defense of
Gericault's principles. It remained for another young
painter to carry on his work after he was gone. The genius
of Delacroix may not have surpassed that of Gericault, but
the way for his progress was already prepared. At the
time David's most illustrious student, Ingres, was startling
Paris by his unmatched draughtsmanship and ability to
reveal character in a portrait by means of the accurate line
of the Florentines, Delacroix revived the romantic spirit of
the Venetians with force and skill. He and Ingres became
the respective champions of Romanticism and Classicism,
just as Ruysdael and Claude had been before them.

The two young painters soon became bitter enemies.

159

Throughout their lives they fought, each in his able way, to uphold the precepts of their art. Victory was inevitable for Delacroix, since the time was ripe for a more virile and imaginative art than the stagnant Classicism of David. And the wave of Romanticism would have swept away the whole antiquated school if it had not been for the single genius of Ingres. It was really not Romanticism against Classicism. It was Romanticism against Ingres.

What were the radical principles which drew so many artists to Delacroix's banner? For one thing he believed that art could not be taught. In this respect he antedated the Modernists. He declared that art was a thing innate in the man, a matter of passion and spirit, and not of rules and craft. He set a premium upon originality, upon the creative instinct; and so his theories came to be interpreted as a defense of novelty. The Academicians even today attribute to him the advent of Modernism, since it was he more than any painter of the early half of the century who denied the principles and traditions of the art.

In his own work he was extremely inventive. His composition went back to the source of all romantic, rhetorical figure arrangement, the Venetians. As for his color, he was perhaps the first Frenchman to see in the landscapes of Constable the beginning of a new era; from the Englishman he derived an appreciation of tone and atmosphere and light. And a certain realism, a dramatic way of presenting ordinary facts, must have filtered through to him from the art of the Spanish realist, Goya.

160

Romanticism to Delacroix meant no more than agitated illustration on a grand scale. There is in his compositions none of the romantic feeling imparted to El Greco's burning canvases for instance; nor is there the quieter romance and drama of Rembrandt's old characters. His romanticism is the romanticism of Rubens—a realistic depiction of events done in exaggerated gestures. But whether or not we thrill to the subjects which thrilled the painter, there remains his leadership of a new and vital cult. Every important movement from his time to Impressionism owes a debt to Delacroix.

The most immediate effect of the Frenchman's energetic campaign for realism was felt among the landscapists. An entire school was founded with him as godfather, Ruysdael as patron saint, and Constable as honorary high priest. The group of painters who settled at Barbizon in the Fontainbleau Forest dedicated their art to atmosphere and the moods of nature. Corot was the outstanding member of this group. Oddly enough, his were the only pictures which retained vestiges of the enemy's methods. In his youth he had learned to people his landscapes with nymphs, cupids and other pagan creatures of fancy. These remnants of a bygone tradition adhered to him but detracted little from his attainments. In his less lyrical subjects, particularly in his pictures of definite places, he loses the fairy-tale quality of his woodland scenes and shows a command of his medium which stamps him a great painter as well as an innovator. (Although Corot's fame rests upon

161

his landscape, critics are gradually coming to the opinion that his figure painting is his greatest form of expression, placing him in a class with Vermeer and Watteau.)

Another type of realism came to light in the work of Millet. Millet was born in Normandy. In spirit as well as geographically he was closer to the Dutch than to the Italians. He was the first French painter of importance to find in the pursuits of the peasant and the laborer, and in their family life, inspiration for pictures. But unlike the genre painters he was not prompted to regard his subjects from the jovial point of view indispensable to the national art of the Netherlands. His peasants are viewed romantically. They have the sadness and fatalistic stamp of Michelangelo's supermen. They are clods, but they are pious and good. They are close to nature, but are her slaves.

As for Millet's manner of painting, it is as simple and as humble as is his subject matter. There is no virtuosity, no evidence of clever brushwork. The paint is simply stuck on. But the solid qualities of form and draughtsmanship ably express his meaning.

His draughtsmanship is not the draughtsmanship of Ingres. Indeed the Barbizon painter's line was as sharp a contrast to the graceful, precise drawing of Ingres as a rustic's honest speech is to the flattery of a courtier. Where Ingres' line fluidly plays about the anatomical swellings and indentations, always subtle and decorative, Millet's, boldly and massively, without regard for detail, expresses

162

the general mood of the figure. Its power and simplicity inspired the satirist Daumier, who ably appropriated the method for his own ends.

The forcefulness of Millet's line seems indicative of his character. He defied academic formulas. He showed how unimportant mere technique or cleverness was when one had something vital to say. He revealed, in his choice of subject, the possibilities of beauty in the most humble and ordinary truths of nature, a plowed field, an old church in the sunlight, a man leaning on a hoe. Finally in his own manner of living he was an inspiration to a whole class of artists who were moved by his example to seek art close to the people instead of in the studios of Montmartre.

Although Millet was an avowed realist, he was, in common with the rest of the Barbizon School though to a lesser degree, a lyricist. The Fontainbleau landscapists all sang the glories of nature. Some frankly drew upon their imaginations, using nature only as a lay model. Monticelli painted fanciful processions that might have taken place a century before. Diaz and Rousseau confined their talents to flaming sunsets and somber foliage. If Millet avoided subjects which obviously bid for sentimental rapture, he yet gave to the most humble scene his poetic commentary.

Classicism had been completely crushed, but now the camp of the Romantics was divided. The Realists seceded. There was a Right Wing and a Left Wing. The radicals believed that the principal aim of their party (and of all painting) was to depict things as they are without comment. Millet, it seemed to them, allowed his poetic emotions to color his presentation of fact. Corot, like the other Barbizon painters, was frankly appealing to our sentimentality. Nature was not all woodland dells with fairy dancers, nor were peasants all patient giants. In some parts of the country peasants were very homely indeed, and not well proportioned. "Let us have the truth," the realists cried. They were influenced of course by the sudden interest in scientific research. It was only a few years before the novelists, Flaubert and Zola, were to show the world how close to actual physical fact literature could get. The romanticism of Victor Hugo was passing out. The prosaic hunters of truth held the field. In their vanguard was the captain of the radical painters, a provincial named Gustave Courbet. A born realist, he had no need for theories. He was destined to influence a later generation as Delacroix had influenced his own.

13

COURBET, WHISTLER
AND MANET

❯❯❯ ❯❯❯ ❮❮❮ ❮❮❮

COURBET, IN a vigorous and crude style of painting which was a little shocking, but none the less effective, strove for a return to nature without the accompaniment of poetry. He wished to be prosaic and literal. He disclaimed any pretension to intellectuality. He declared that he was not familiar with classical lore and that never having seen a man with wings, could not paint angels. The romanticism of Delacroix bored him. He was only a painter, he protested, not a story teller.

In reality his art is of that subtle, imaginative brand possessed by Rembrandt. The noisy overabundant gesturing of Delacroix would have annoyed Rembrandt as much as it did Courbet. The sensitive painter who wishes to express only truth will present that facet of truth which is lit up by his own keen unliterary imagination. In spite of all Courbet's protestations for an impersonal, calm, detached, scientific observation of objects and affairs he was innately a dramatist with the restraint of Giotto, a character analyst with the incisiveness of Rembrandt and Leonardo. The eminent French critic Mauclair says of him: "His astonishing psychological studies of faces are worthy of the most perfect modern pages of Flaubert, and correspond precisely with the impression which Madame Bovary produced in French literature in the face of sentimental romance. Such a painter has nothing in common with the realism which followed in his name. He saw *true* and not *exact;* his work is not a painted photograph, a dry, useless copy of obvious details. It is bathed in golden light and warm shadows, it presents the larger aspects of nature, it moves us by its superb mastery."

Nevertheless Courbet was more objective than the Dutch. Where the Dutch painters sought for the beauty in unimportant objects, more often than otherwise *giving* beauty to them by deft handling and understanding of atmospheric light, Courbet painted without any attempt to add charm by cleverness or skill. Much of his landscape is even ugly, just as many spots in nature are ugly. For this reason his

166

work is distasteful to those who think it is the business of the artist to *refine* nature or to present only her better moods and aspects.

Assuredly Courbet's paintings are not distinguished by any lofty or profound thought. They are not spiritual in the sense that Giorgione's are for instance, nor are they motivated by any sentiment, religious, human, romantic. Their worth lies in the impression of power, in the *painting qualities* which leap from the canvas. His paintings are beautiful, not by reason of their message, but by their force and great, almost moral, sincerity.

In the face of all sorts of discouragement, rejections by official exhibition juries, the raillery of the public, the attacks of critics, he continued to paint his "Copies of Nature." Discouragement only served to hold him to his purpose. He was by temperament a revolutionist. And not only did he stand by his guns as an artist, but such was his political radicalism that the government found it expedient to exile him from France in his later years.

By his crusading spirit and persistency in his course Courbet established a point of view which years later affected a group of painters of real and vital ability: the Post-Impressionists. The experiments of Cezanne, whose studio was a laboratory for the production of beauty by color, form and space, are largely the outgrowth of Courbet's new approach. The latter's *Man with the Pipe* led to many men with pipes by the master of Aix. The buxom nudes (painted for form and not illustration) that shocked the French public of 1850 and 1860 because they did not conform to the svelte type popular among Frenchmen, served as models to the greatest of all painters of nudes, Renoir. Courbet was, therefore, the forerunner of Modernist figure painters.

If he was slow in awakening Paris to the value of his point of view, it was partly because sophisticated Parisians found it difficult to take a rough provincial seriously. It remained to his most promising pupil to take up cudgels in his defense—and the only cudgels effective were the bitter polemics smart people can understand. Edouard Manet was a person of the proper background to meet critics and society on their own field. Just as in London the American painter Whistler brilliantly defended his art by attacking his clumsy critics, so Manet belabored the Philistines with the sharp blade of his vocabulary. He wrote and talked and enlisted in his cause the service of literary celebrities.

In spite of his energetic defense of his art, or perhaps because of it, he was denounced even more than his teacher had been. His pictures were thrown out of exhibitions by members of the Academy who saw their institution reduced to impotence by his daring attacks and brilliant masterpieces. Many considered him a madman because he painted a group of his friends picnicking in the woods in the company of a nude young lady. Life for a time was an incessant battle, a series of insults, hoots and attacks by journalists. But with the exhibition of his *Olympia* (Fig. 27) it became evident to Parisians that, criticize as they might, they

168

numbered among them a genius of the first rank. Manet became celebrated. Young art students recognized his dominance in matters of art; they forsook the schools for his guidance. With their defection official French painting passed into a secondary position where it has remained to this day.

There are several periods in Manet's work. Courbet taught him, but his youthful nature responded to the drama of Goya. Spain lured him. Spanish life fascinated him. For a time young Manet devoted his talents to the painting of bullfights and toreadors and Spanish dancers. His travels always left vivid impressions upon him, so that Spain affected him romantically while Italy awakened in him a religious spirit. There was a period in which he painted pictures of Christ. Finally the influence of the Dutch School made itself felt and he struck his proper stride. Impressed by Rembrandt's point of view, he decided to place character above everything else. He discovered in himself a certain Rembrandtesque ability to express the traits of people in portraits. And to better attain a positivity of statement, he eliminated every detail unnecessary to his purpose. He worked with a large brush, in great flat masses, with the sharp values (the distinct black and white) of the Spaniards.

But instead of making his masses melt into each other, in the manner of Velasquez and Goya, he introduced, with the aid of Whistler, a new treatment. He kept his darks and lights in sharp decorative patterns linked with each other,

169

or "tied together." Raphael had innovated this system of pattern in European painting, as we saw in his School of Athens. But Manet and Whistler carried it to a degree of breadth and simplification that plainly derived from the Japanese print. The pictorial pattern of the Japanese had always been prized by European connoisseurs; but no one suspected that it could be incorporated in Western art. With characteristic dash and defiance, the two painters successfully applied it to their work.

Let us leave Manet for a moment to speak of his contemporary, Whistler, the legends of whose wit and eccentricities have served to obscure somewhat his greater significance as a painter. His exact place in the history of painting has not yet been established. American by birth and English by adoption, he remains essentially French by virtue of his training in art and his own predisposition for the French point of view or attitude. Most English and American painters who are French taught, once they are out of Paris, quickly return to their native traditions. They go to Paris in the first place to learn *how a thing is done,* not *what is worth doing.* Whistler was unlike them. Because he adhered to the French tradition, not to the Anglo-Saxon (advertisement of the subject, sentiment, or moral and social propaganda), his name belongs beside Manet's.

In actual sparkle of performance, Manet surpassed Whistler. The American had learned his art by careful study of Velasquez. The Spanish master's subtly painted heads taught him an appreciation for soft modeling and

170

for nuances in flesh tones. Manet, as we have seen, was in his maturity inspired by Rembrandt. The Dutch master was more dramatic, and drama in any form appealed to the Frenchman. So that when the two painters startled Paris by their Japanese design, the restrained and sensitive Whistler seemed a mild rebel in comparison with the bold Manet.

The very range of Manet's versatility detracts from his character as a painter. Whatever style or subject he attempted he executed with distinction; but no sooner had he demonstrated his mastery of a particular kind of painting than he was off on a new tack. The feverish urge to startle the public must have been brought about largely by a defiance toward a hostile reception of anything coming from his brush. Where many painters succumb to mediocrity by trying to please their public, Manet ran the risk of weakening his powers by trying to shock his public.

The *Olympia* referred to is an apt illustration of both his brilliance and his defiance of public conventions. The picture follows closely one of Titian's celebrated compositions in which a nude lies outstretched upon her bed. For his nude, Manet selected a well-known sophisticated society woman and gave her face an expression of quizzical boredom. The atmospheric subtlety of Titian's picture is discarded. The bold flat masses are as striking as his model. While the realism of the scene grips us, the literary quality of the picture is obvious; it is even shocking litera-

171

ture and as such responsible for the animosity of critics. But no one can deny that it is great painting.

The stir occasioned by his *Olympia* moved Manet to an even more dashing way of painting. He developed a short-cut technique that seemed inspired by a kind of braggadocio, an effort to surpass Hals in economy of means. By a few deft strokes he was able to recreate the person or scene before him. This deftness eventually became the systematized sleight of hand of Carolus Duran, and of the latter's pupil, Sargent. But where Manet's genius, like Rembrandt's, lay in his psychological ability to ferret out the secrets of one's character, the later experts made smartness of technique the end of art.

By going beyond the simplified brushwork of Franz Hals, Manet virtually established impressionism. The well-placed stroke supplanted conscientious modeling; it was able to *suggest* an entire surface, a figure, or a mass of moving figures.

The appeal of this sort of impressionism is readily apparent. The charm lies in its vaudeville qualities. You walk close to the canvas and see only a blob. You step back and there, as real as life, is a moving figure. Now you see it, now you don't. How is it done?

Manet was the first impressionist, yet he does not belong to that group officially known as Impressionists. The latter were his own pupils. But they were motivated by aims entirely different from his own.

172

PART THREE

꘎꘎꘎꘎

The Evolution of Modern Art

35. STILL LIFE—BRAQUE

36. STILL LIFE—PICASSO

37. THE CART—ROUSSEAU

38. SAINTE-SEVERIN CHURCH—UTRILLO

14

THE IMPRESSIONISTS

⇒⇒⇒-⇒⇒⇒-⇐⇐⇐-⇐⇐

AT THE time the illustrious Manet was shocking and defying the critics and the bourgeois with his daring pictures, Europe was thrilling to the discoveries of science. France, as the newspapers might have expressed it, was becoming "science conscious." Pasteur and his pupil, Metchnikoff, were holding the interest of the public. It was only a few years before Edison was to startle the Paris Exposition with his phonograph, and the whole world with his incandescent lamp. Literature, as we have seen, followed along, led by Zola, Flaubert, the Goncourt brothers, and others less distinguished. Music was experimenting with new combinations and harmonies, the innovations of the German, Wagner, serving to goad young composers to cold laboratory research in sounds. It remained only for painting to enlist under the banner of the scientists.

Courbet, alone among the painters of his time, had foreseen the new trend a generation earlier. Young painters now turned back to his work. There was nothing in it as dazzling as Manet's virtuosity, but its point of view was in keeping with the new objectivity. The question was: Could painters go beyond Courbet in scientific approach? Would they have to examine nature through miscroscopes as Zola was doing in his writings? The musicians indicated a different direction. They dealt with new combinations of notes. Why not new combinations of color? Color was the unexplored field. The Englishman Turner had left the world amazing watercolor sketches of a brilliance and light and intensity unmatched in the history of painting. Who knew what secrets color would yield if approached scientifically? Young painters began a laboratory investigation of color.

They discovered certain truths. For example, shadow or darkness was not the absence of light, outdoors, but only a different colored light. If the sun shone on a dirt road the road appeared yellow. If a house or tree threw a shadow across the road, the shadow was not brown nor an

176

indiscriminate dark, but was just as light as the yellow sunlight; only it was the opposite color, violet.

Again they discovered that there was no such thing as color *belonging* to an object, or *local* color. A table was not gray or brown. The light reflected on the table made it appear gray or brown. Optical science taught that the light reflects upon the retina of the eye, the human lens, and causes a particular color to appear, depending upon the number or frequency of vibrations. We see things red, green or yellow not because there are such colors, but because the eye receives certain vibrations. These in turn depend upon the quality of the light which surfaces reflect.

If we walk up to a tree it appears green. If we stand off from the tree and half close our eyes to shut out distracting detail, we see the sunlit foliage yellow and the shadows a brilliant blue. The light reflected by the leaves gives them their color.

Constable revealed the charm and reality of atmosphere. He showed that the condition of the air and the time of day altered the color of objects. The scientific painters seized upon this theory also. So that between reflected light and atmosphere, local color was thrown over as an illusion and deception.

But these are not all of the discoveries. Outline was shown not to exist in nature. It was an artifice that indicated where two masses, each of different color, came together. If the color matched nature accurately, why have outline? And as for the masses of color they only appear

177

red or yellow or green, because they reflect with greater or less frequency, as has been said. In reality all masses of color, except the pure or primary colors, red, yellow and blue, are composed of all the colors in the rainbow; gray consists of spots of every color as does brown. The difference in their appearance is the result only of the proportionate number of color atoms. For example, green appears green because there are more blue and yellow spots apparent in it than any other spots. If all spots were present in an equal proportion we should have the white light of the prism. When we mix our pigments equally, however, we do not attain this white light because the body of the pigment deadens the color, the luminosity. Instead we get brown. Any color *except* red, yellow, and blue, the Impressionists discovered, is composed of spots of red, yellow and blue and any of their combinations.

The net result of all this scientific investigation was to make painters turn their backs on museums and art schools and devote their talents to catching upon canvas the fugitive accidents of nature. The way in which fleeting light affected the *surface* color was the object of their studies. Form was forgotten. Composition was reduced to the most simple arrangement. The scientist-painters devoted themselves entirely to watching the changes of nature.

Claude Monet was the leader of these innovators. He was an able artist besides being a hardworking one. He went out into a field and painted a hay-stack at nine o'clock, again at ten-thirty, and still again at twelve, in order to

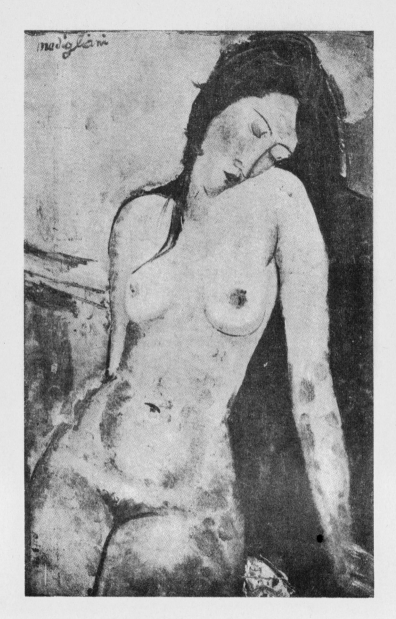

39. NUDE—MODIGLIANI

40. GIRL ROWING — GROMAIRE

show how the little specks or atoms of color in the hay changed from hour to hour. It mattered little that his subject was a stack of hay. It could just as well have been a bale of spinach.

To the Salon in Paris of 1863, Monet sent a picture of a sunset. In that year the authorities were generous enough to hang in one gallery all the rejected pictures, and the sunset was one of them. The jokers and wags had a pleasurable time in this room at the expense of the unlucky artists. They stopped to examine the new color analysis in Monet's sunset and noted the title: *Impression.* From that time on, the name Impressionism was given to the work of the scientific colorists who painted all things in spots of pure color, or component elements of a color.

The word Impressionist was really a misnomer. Manet with his dashing portraits and nudes was more an impressionist than any of these colorists. The famous Sargent, who could make one stroke take the place of nine, was certainly so. Whistler's nocturnes were the very essence of impressionism. But none of these painters are today included among the Impressionists. The industrious, meticulous color analyzers attempted to dissect nature by formula and actually permitted themselves no impressions at all. Yet a freak of fortune dubbed them all by that name.

The most astounding thing about the scientist-painters is that they attracted to their cold researches in color the most tender and poetic artists: lyricists and sentimentalists. The lacy sylvan dells of Corot were translated literally

179

into the new color systems. Impressionism gradually swung into a dreamy pursuit of *nuances*, little changes in harmonies of color; this effeminacy was reflected in the poetry of the period, and even more in the music. We have only to listen to a composition of Debussy to be aware of the whole movement of the Impressionists toward odd little harmonies, exquisitely sweet, but devoid of any classical construction.

The period, however much it tended to decadence, was not fruitless. It contributed to painting that understanding of color and color relationship which we have discussed. And in its principal exponent, Claude Monet, it left the world a great painter and artist.

Let us look at his painting *The Staircase* (Fig. 28). The black and white reproduction is not accurate in values, since the camera makes black whatever is painted orange and red. But the general characteristics of the painting are not entirely lost. We note first of all the airiness or atmosphere that pervades the picture. There are no sharp lines. The roof and walls are bathed in mellow sunlight so there is no possibility of pattern. Severe geometric areas are sacrificed to tonal diffusion.

Yet we cannot say that the picture is disorganized or unorganized. By a well-thought-out distribution of dark accents or spots the canvas is given balance. Each dark complements another. The rectangular areaway on the left is opposed by the decorative lines of the two young trees on the right which follow each other in rhythmic grace. The

180

focal point of the picture, the head of the stairway, is marked by a note of dark in just the right place, not *too near* the center of the canvas.

The qualities of form and spacial relation, however, are nowhere apparent. The roof does not slant back, the stairs do not run away from us. You cannot walk into the areaway. The foliage is not massive.

There is no pretension to these classical qualities because they are outside the tenets of the Impressionists. Monet preferred to paint foliage shimmering rather than massive, so that "birds can fly through it." There is no denying the gentle charm of this unweighty, unrigid painting. The pliable pigment and delicate brushstroke are made the vehicles of a lyrical feeling for sun and air. In addition to these attributes the scintillating color is of such a quality as to insure the validity of the picture on that score alone. Unfortunately this "scientific" color has inspired countless imitators with no ability whatever beyond a shrewdness for dissecting and aping the method.

The names of two other Impressionists are generally linked with Monet. Camille Pissaro, a Portuguese Jew, was the real theorist of the group. While his own pictures have not the intensity achieved by Monet, his range is wider. He was by nature the true impressionist, in the sense that Manet was. A quick dab of color suggested life and movement to him. By means of variegated spots he was able to catch the illusion of moving crowds, the bustle of a Paris street. The very lack of definition created a rapidity of movement that literal painting could never attain.

The Englishman Sisley was the third eminent member of the group. His work betrays his racial origin. The lyrical attitude becomes at times cloyingly sweet, but there is no denying the delicacy of nuance and the fascination of his sensitive brushwork. In his landscapes surface prettiness is stressed out of all proportion to the art qualities. To him can be attributed the English and American tendencies in academic landscape painting.

Monet, Pissaro and Sisley remain the distinguished triumvirate of Impressionism. In spite of the fact that the new theories and formulas tended to make painting foolproof—"any child can work it"—these are the only names written in the history of the movement. It is true the Impressionists counted in their number the great master Degas, but Degas was an aloof genius whose personal power was greater than theories.

We shall devote little time to Degas as our interest is chiefly centered upon innovators in painting and not upon practitioners, however great their talent. There are many volumes dealing with Degas' art and his pictures are widely scattered in the museums. The spectator will see in his work all the classical qualities but so subservient will they appear to the artist's sharp observation that his personality or *significance* will dominate the canvas. When Berenson places him in the company of Rembrandt and Velasquez he exaggerates only slightly. For Degas pos-

182

sessed the power of presenting the salient, visual facts of
back-stage life, the race track environment, and the humble
gestures and bodies of working women with the realism of
Velasquez and the dramatic force of Rembrandt. His portraits rank with the ablest. But since he is not primarily
an Impressionist we must leave further eulogy of his talents
to others.

We spoke before of the widespread interest in painting
brought about by the Impressionist formula. What was
this formula? It consisted mainly of two precepts, or more
properly, recipes. First, everything was to be painted in
pure colors; no browns, nor blacks, nor grays were per-
missible since these colors were composed of atoms of
red, yellow, blue, violet, orange and green. Second, whatever was touched by sunlight was yellow, while shadow
was blue or violet. A road was yellow in sunlight and blue
in shadow. A tree was also yellow in sunlight and blue in
shadow. A spot of red judiciously placed tended to relieve
a picture of its monotony. To see the practical appli-
cation of this formula we have only to visit an artists'
colony in the summer and watch the hundreds of amateurs
at work. The scene which meets their eye is translated into
the terms of their formula. Thus art becomes in their hands
a kind of domestic science. An enormous amount of con-
coctions have been created in the name of Monet since his
acceptance by official art circles.

Naturally the dignity of the profession of painting was
for a time wiped out by the rush of amateurs who were

183

eager to have a fling at the new formula. Painting became as popular a sport in Paris as cycling. And this popularity was exploited by a new type of artist, the business-artist, or interior decorator. He understood the problem of cheering people up by means of bright colors. The whole democratic movement of the last thirty years towards colors, meaningless, inane, but *pretty*, comes from Impressionism.

We must see, however, that Impressionism aided the development of modern painting in two ways. First it contributed a scientific understanding of color, and second, it disgusted, with its inanity, those virile artists who required a personal method of expression. These came to be called the Post-Impressionists. They were as hardy a lot of painters as has been seen since the Renaissance.

41. HYMN TO BEAUTY—GROSZ

42. PORTRAIT—SOUTINE
Collection — John F. Kraushaar

modeled with the simplicity of a figure by Giotto. And in other respects too, he shows his heritage of Renaissance art. The languid, sad poses of his Tahitian people are not unlike those of Perugino's wistful worshipers. Finally in his use of decorative line, abstract, flowing, beautiful without being a part of a beautiful person, he reveals another debt to Botticelli.

Yet in spite of Gauguin's appropriation of Florentine methods, he wishes to be simple and primitive. He inculcates into his figures a savage mysticism. He copies their odd proportions and gestures. He records the pristine state of their society. He is somber, poetic, faithful to his adopted countrymen. If he fails in achieving completely the primitive's emotional attitude, it is because he can not shake off the vestiges of Paris and his early training. His suavity of line and richness of color betray his superior knowledge and sensual refinement. The point of view is primitive but the spectacles are those of a sophisticated man of the world.

Nevertheless the unswerving ideals of the painter speak from his canvases. Coming in the fading hours of anæmic Impressionism his truthfulness is not only refreshing, it falls like a bomb among the painters of pretty spots. He may not be the true primitive, but he is civilized *enough* to be aware of the true primitive's superior mode of living. "Sound art," he seems to be always repeating, "can derive only from a people whose hearts are fresh and unsullied." How unlike the duplicity of the knavish yet kindly Perugino.

187

The Dutch painter Van Gogh was as colorful a character as the picturesque Gauguin. An extremely sensitive, neurotic man, he was overwhelmed by the difficulties of living and eventually went mad. His art was the product of his spontaneous reactions, not of theories. Yet few painters have exerted their influence upon a younger generation as has this unbalanced Dutchman. While Cezanne is accredited with the innovation which gave the greatest impulse *technically* to modern painting, it was Van Gogh who effected the change in the point of view *esthetically*. That is to say, he opened the eyes of painters, as well as of the public, to the beauty of homely and hitherto-considered-ugly things.

We have seen how humble was his quest for the beauty in simple things. A chair was worthy of a portrait, as was an old pair of shoes or a brown deserted battlefield. His nervous, sketchy, fervid haste detracts nothing from the force of the message he wishes to convey. On the contrary, his pictures seem the result of sudden discoveries and impetuous effort to fix them upon canvas. Something about a scene or object or person swiftly revealed itself to him and inspired him to paint. The swirling brushwork betrays his impatience to record the character of his object.

As a portraitist he descends from Rembrandt. His quest is for the character of his sitter. The nuances of flesh tones and the cleverness of the brushwork do not entice him. This is clear when we compare his work to that of the smart practitioner. Our late Sargent painted all heads in much the same accomplished manner. If he pictured a peasant he had only to put a white collar about the sunburnt neck to metamorphose the rustic into a statesman or business executive. When Van Gogh painted a peasant it was not only the whole race of peasantry that he caught on his canvas, but the idiosyncrasies of the individual. His man could be no other. This is apparent in his portrait of the *Man With the Red Hair* (Fig. 30). The honesty and discernment of the painter startle us. He shows that he is not befuddled by civilized notions of how a man *should* look.

His landscapes, however, reveal more of his mental and emotional states than do his interiors, portraits and still-life studies. Confronted with nature, a slushy street, old houses, a barren field, hospital grounds, he attains a kind of wild lyricism which takes us out of ourselves. There is a religious fanaticism in his painting of a tree or sky. He is no longer the keen eye searching to record the salient facts of a man's character. He is no longer objective. All his pent up emotional mysticism escapes him. When he paints his swirling sunsets, he is praying to his God. He is another Fra Angelico.

Just as Gauguin's life in Tahiti explains the man's art, so do the facts of Van Gogh's brief and stormy existence throw some light upon his painting. That his father was a Calvinist minister is itself important. The early religious environment deeply affected the boy, whether or not he inherited the temperament of a shepherd of humanity. At sixteen he was working in the shop of his uncle, a picture

189

dealer. The love of art was here instilled in him. He devoted himself to drawing and painting with such seriousness that we find him at the youthful age of twenty-three an art teacher in Ramsgate, England. Then suddenly the urge to minister to the spiritual needs of his fellow men comes upon him. Freud might find in this urge to preach the same fundamental causes as in the urge to paint—a moral and emotional, perhaps sexual conflict. Whatever the reason, he returned to Amsterdam to study theology. He became imbued with ideas of Christian communism, a sort of nostalgia for the life of the Catacombs. He went to live with a company of coal miners. But he did not preach to them for long. His own salvation seemed possible only in the realm of art. Painting lured him away from his mission. With his brother Theo he went to Paris. Theo found employment in the galleries of the famous Goupil and was soon able to introduce Vincent to painters of the first rank. The erstwhile missionary became a convert to their doctrines. He reveled in the brilliant color of the Impressionists and the later theorists. Seurat's method of painting with spots of pure pigment intrigued him. It was Gauguin, however, who captivated his romantic nature. The young Dutchman discarded the browns and blacks of his countrymen and experimented with color—luminous, pure, intense color. Then Paris palled on him.

He settled at Arles, in Provence, in February, 1888. He found the soft sunshine and the open country an Arcadia after the café life of drizzly Paris. Yet he missed

190

his friends. He urged Gauguin to join him. The older painter came and together they established a *ménage*. Once his companion was with him, however, life was not smooth. The irritable, touchy nature of the neurotic Dutchman provoked many quarrels. On one occasion he threatened Gauguin with a knife and then, overcome with repentance, did what is his most celebrated act, cut off his own ear. He was taken to a hospital. When he returned his mind was definitely shaken. He was soon back in the infirmary, this time never to leave. The remainder of his short life was spent under the shadow of insanity. But he continued to paint. Painting calmed him. He expended his emotion with the act of putting paint on canvas. The masterpieces of this period sing with his spiritual excitement. Yet painting was not release enough. On July 29, 1890, at the age of thirty-seven, he shot himself dead.

The progress of Van Gogh's art as well as his mental and nervous disintegration is marked by his technique or brushwork, the handwriting of the painter. In his early Paris period the strokes are calm, studied, regular, not particularly arresting. Later they are stylized into the vertical and the horizontal. But after a short time at Arles his manner changes. He becomes nervous, impatient, the result, as some historians say, of overwork and sunstroke. His emotional unrest is reflected in a less laborious, rapid, sometimes furious technique. The mental disturbance is accompanied by a swirling, ecstatic brushwork.

His painting may be divided into the Gauguin period,

191

in which his pattern and color are the most interesting qualities, and into the period of the full attainment of his own powers. Again it may be separated into the product of his objective state of mind in which he presents us the curious facts of nature's most humble objects, and into that of his subjective state of mind in which he painted pæans of praise to God. In either state he is a master. But in the first he contributes something for others to follow; in the second he stands alone, a spiritual, hysterical poet and prophet of the Lord.

In contrast to Van Gogh, Cezanne's contributions to painting lie not so much in his spiritual force or outlook as in his command of the qualities of the art itself. He taught form through the use of planes of contrasting color. And by the same means he attained a remarkable sense of space or spatial relation, as we have already seen in the landscape in Chapter 3. If we compare this landscape with the painting by Perugino, we get an idea of the different methods employed by the two foremost masters of space composition. The Cezanne loses much of its power when reduced to black and white since it is largely from the warm and cool hues that the effect is obtained. But even so, it is readily apparent that Perugino's space is accomplished by treating his figures as masses placed in a particular atmosphere which fades lighter and lighter as it goes back, while Cezanne's space is the result of planes of color. This color leads us across one flat stretch or area and starts us again on the one beyond. In Perugino's pictures we travel smoothly and continuously into the distance. In Cezanne's we negotiate one section at a time.

Cezanne was a less inspired but steadier worker than Van Gogh. His painting was extremely long in evolving. While the influences of many painters had served others, Manet for instance, by developing their skill, virtuosity and versatility, Cezanne's progress was retarded by his too eager admiration for popular artists. His personality was therefore slow in developing. For a time his ambition was to have his pictures hung in the same gallery with the work of Bougereau, a miscast photographer who thrilled the literal-minded by his uninspired renditions of nature's details. It required a lifetime of effort for Cezanne to work out his own artistic salvation. And just as his taste was late in maturing, so was his command of the medium laboriously accomplished. To his old age he retained crudities of brushwork. Van Gogh, writing to a friend of the old man's difficulties in technique, very charitably attributed them to Cezanne's shaky easel. He wrote:

"Let us drop the word clumsy, since it is possible he painted these outdoor studies while the wind was blowing. Having had the same difficulty often myself, I find this the explanation for his brushstrokes being sometimes very sure and at other times seemingly clumsy. It's his easel which shakes in the wind."

Fortunately for Cezanne and the world at large, economic security enabled him to take his time in maturing. The modest income which he inherited permitted him

193

to leave distracting Paris and withdraw to his native Provence, not far from Arles where Van Gogh painted. Oblivious to critics, fads, and popular demands, he worked away zealously. Painting was a passion to him in spite of his difficulties in expressing himself. And if he repainted a canvas forty times before he was satisfied with its beginning, in his mind he knew what he wished to achieve. A hundred years before him Watteau had hit upon the principle of color contrasts. Cezanne devoted his life to the pursuit of a similar color formula to aid him in expressing form and space. In spirit, then, he is completely removed from Gauguin and Van Gogh; and in spite of his quest for the most desirable of all painting qualities, form, he is temperamentally close to the first Impressionists, the scientists with paint. He himself expressed his ambitions most clearly when he said: "I want to make of Impressionism something as durable as the art of the museums."

If Van Gogh is inimitable because of the spirit and personality which dominate his pictures, Cezanne is the very opposite. It is obvious that every formula presupposes imitation. The Cezanne formula is taught in art schools as the Impressionist formula was taught ten years ago. Cezannism is degenerating like Impressionism. The technique of the master is copied but the problem which inspired him is being forgotten. This is inevitable where a formula promises fool-proof art.

The artists who really profited by Cezanne's experiments were not his imitators but those who were alive to the

194

43. THE ANNIVERSARY—CHAGALL

44. I AND THE VILLAGE—CHAGALL

importance of his principles. The Cubists, as we shall see, detached the various planes and forms and lines from the objects to which they belonged and rearranged them in arbitrary compositions. We can attribute to Cezanne the germ of this Modernist movement in painting.

It was not from Cezanne alone, however, that the Cubists learned of the possibilities of geometric forms. Seurat was a painter of greater intellect than the master of Aix-en-Provence. His pictures are mathematical, devoid of the sensuous quality present in Cezanne's work. The forms of his figures are reduced to geometric patterns. There is an attempt at form, very subtle, but in most cases successful. The color is that of the Impressionists broken into spots like Monet's and applied to the canvas in rigid little dots; so that any suggestion of freedom, even in the brushwork, is absent. Seurat knew the values of color as a lexicographer knows the values of words.

In the picture reproduced, *The Circus* (Fig. 31), we see how every intricate form has been reduced to the most simple conventional pattern. This intellectual, formal kind of painting is often referred to, or spoken of, as the art of the museum, something that Impressionism with its lack of design and form was not. The Cubists appropriated Seurat's geometry and combined it with Cezanne's planes, as we shall see.

Renoir had no theories. He was a genius in the art of imbuing his figures, particularly his nudes, with a lifelike vitality absent in Seurat as well as in the Impressionists.

195

While his paintings are the most normally satisfying of this period of innovation and revolt, his point of view is the same old-fashioned one which Titian and Rubens possessed some three and a half centuries before. He does, in fact, show the influences of these masters in many ways. His color, for example, is warm and rich like theirs. But not even they can match him in the painting of scintillant flesh. Early training as a ceramist taught him facts about color as it had taught Gauguin. Where other able painters thought of the canvas as a support or background for the paint, Renoir *used its whiteness* as a base; so that by keeping his color thin and fairly transparent he attained the ceramist's luminosity.

Volume or form was, however, his own special preoccupation. None of the inflated nudes of Rubens is as convincingly real as are Renoir's. We have seen in the nude in Chapter 3 with what subtlety, yet with what conviction he was able to create the illusion of round forms.

It is evident that Renoir loved to paint nudes, as Van Gogh loved to paint a field or tree. One was a sensualist, the other a passionate mystic. One calm, a gourmet enjoying the refractions of light upon pink flesh and the perfect modeling of a young girl's body, the other looking at nature with a wild, chaotic appreciation of her mystic beauty. Renoir may have loved women as much as Casanova loved them but what he has put down on canvas was the charm of light falling upon woman's skin, and the volume or form over her skeleton. When he painted a nude,

196

in other words, he was mainly painter, somewhat poet—but not just man.

He had no intellectual theories to offer the young students who thrilled to his pictures. It is told of him that he could not tolerate art writers, critics, and the painting phrases which they carelessly flung about. Once when entering a tobacco shop he was at a loss to know what brand of cigar to choose. He read the names on the boxes: "Colorado," "Claro." "There," he said, "is the whole science of painting, colorado and claro."

If Renoir formulated no new systems his influence was none the less marked. He could not tell one how to paint, he could not bring science into his service as Monet had; nor apply Seurat's geometry to painting, nor explain the psychological reasons for Cezanne's astounding theories; but he could indicate a road to travel, a point of view to take. His pictures restored the art of nude-painting to its proper position and inspired a productivity in that branch which has resulted in its becoming a principal subject for modern painters. The Autumn Salon in Paris and the Independents show hundreds of nudes each year, many of them painted from the objective point of view of Renoir. The vogue of fat, "repulsive" women can be attributed to him more than to any other painter, since artists learned from his pictures that beauty depends upon the ability to record the form and light, not upon the pulchritude of the model.

In contrast to the aims of Renoir were the ideals and motives of Odilon Redon. This little known painter is of tremendous importance historically. Born in the same year as Renoir, 1841, he remained aloof from Impressionism, Post-Impressionism and their various doctrines. He was not properly a painter. He was a poet who invaded the field of the painter, carrying to it the poetic currents of the day, Symbolism and Mysticism. The influence of Poe, Verlaine and Baudelaire marks his every conception. Baudelaire may have helped shape his destiny when he wrote as early as 1859, "From day to day art is losing respect for itself and is prostrating itself before exterior reality. The artist is more and more inclined to paint, not what he dreams, but what he sees. . . . Whatever is created by the spirit is more vital than matter."

This essence of the spirit Redon attempted to express with paint. Critics looked with suspicion upon his efforts. Are not symbols for ideas and emotions hieroglyphics rather than the painter's art? they asked. They ignored his work and so failed to see the inception of a point of view which has steadily invaded all Europe. For Redon's painted dreams not only inspired the tender symbolism of Gauguin but opened the way for a later generation of Expressionists and Surrealists. Nearly every subjective painter of today in some way owes a debt to this lone explorer of an uncharted sea.

198

16

THE FAUVES AND CUBISTS

⇛⇛⇚⇚

THE PATHS hewn by the Post-Impressionists through the jungle of pretty-colored art were broadened by their zestful pupils and successors. About 1905 a group of these young followers, thrown together mainly by their studies in the atelier of Gustave Moreau and by their café meetings, thrashed out the new ideas and set themselves the tasks of carrying them to their ultimate destination. They banded themselves into a little society hoping perhaps to find renown, like courage, in numbers. They aimed to shock

Paris and better to do so took the terrifying name "Les Fauves" (The Wild Beasts). These wild beasts numbered among them such gentle and genial souls as Derain, Matisse, Braque, Friesz, Dufy and Vlaminck.*

To understand what the Fauves contributed to the art of painting it is necessary to keep before us the achievements of their predecessors. We have seen that Gauguin, besides revealing the possibilities of decorative pattern and color relations, showed that linear beauty (decorative line) could be derived from an ill-proportioned people, as well as from the classical figures of Greek sculpture.

The Fauves studied Gauguin's color relations and discovered that they were beautiful even when not confined to definite patterns. Masses of color, however indeterminate in shape, could be harmoniously composed. Line was beautiful in itself too and had no need for color to support its decorative quality. In short, the Fauves separated the two elements.

Instead of painting a nude flesh color and marking the boundaries of the color by the outline, as painters had always done, they introduced whatever other hue seemed

---

* Vlaminck in his recent autobiography attributes the birth of Fauvism to the accident of his meeting Derain. He says,... "A scandal struck the artistic world, a universal laugh went up from the public when it saw, hung on the panels of the Cours-la-Reine barracks, the canvases of André Derain and myself.... There were adversaries, partisans, and the second year, disciples. In the same place were reunited the artists of this tendency (the tendency to work in great splashes of pure color) which was dubbed by one of our comrades 'fauvisme.'"

effective as decoration. One side of a woman's leg might be green, the other side pink. Viewed abstractly the painting was alive with harmonious color relations that were completely free of the boundaries imposed by outline. Line too was freed of its slavish imitation of nature. Just as Botticelli had made his pictures seductive by rhythm of line, so the Fauves attempted to secure a decorative charm by the same means. But where the Florentine had been subtle, involved, the shocking Parisians tried to be extremely simple, even brutal in the manner of the Byzantines.

Byzantine art was seized upon by the back-to-the-elemental painter. Indeed, any primitive art was inspiration to the Fauves quite as much as was the work of the Post-Impressionists. Even the distortion of Van Gogh, which played upon the emotions so effectively, was found to have its origin in the work of the early Christians.

In the search for new savage expression the art of the negro was discovered. Painters avidly examined the masks, textiles, weapons and statuettes of the Congo for new forms and lines. They made a fetish of fetishes.

What was it the Fauves sought in the art of primitive peoples? Was it the emotional quality absent from civilized art? Was it the expression of terror, lust, the superstitious or religious urge? Only in a few rare instances. For the most part the young heroes were too sophisticated to be touched by the elemental emotions of uncivilized peoples.

201

They sought what they were able to appreciate: new principles of decoration.

*   *   *

MATISSE is an outstanding member of the Fauves. He has done with color what his revolutionary contemporaries in music have done with chords. He has put colors together which before his successful efforts were considered impossible to harmonize. Some critics have expressed their belief that he derived his astounding color sense from study of the design of Persians and Hindoos. But the succession of new arrangements in his canvases has established beyond question his originality as a composer of harmonies. While he is preëminent as a colorist, his work does not affect us deeply or hold our attention for long. Its weakness is due to its strength. In other words, his painting is excellent decoration, but too often remains only that. In the picture we reproduce (Fig. 32), we see how much he has simplified the lady and the chair, and how he has selected and stressed those particular lines which give them a decorative rhythm. Deprived of the brilliant, exotic color the reproduction seems more of a sketch than a painting. The whole thing has been reduced to a system of decoration, pleasing to the eye, but possessing neither the form nor the character of the woman and chair. The point of view is detached and impersonal, yet it is special rather than objective. It is a selective *extraction of decorative lines* combined with the artist's feeling for color.

202

45. PENZBERG — CAMPENDONCK

When we say that his pictures are primarily decoration we do not mean that they are altogether devoid of emotional content. Everything the artist *sees* for the first time excites him as a child is excited by new experiences, and this excitement is, if the painter is capable, transferred to the spectator. Matisse has succeeded beyond most painters in translating into color the quick reaction to the object.* But in no sense, except perhaps that of color, has he surpassed the Post-Impressionists, particularly Van Gogh, in expressing this rapid emotional reaction to the object.

These principles of Matisse were carried to their logical conclusion by Raoul Dufy. In his earlier landscapes he discarded formal notions of design or composition which demand unity, which require a single center of interest, and extracted the decorative elements of whatever met his gaze. Watercolor seemed more suitable to his fragmentary pursuit of pretty little nuances. He sought out the different decorative *motifs*, the checks, loops, circles, and so on. There is unquestionably a design, but it is the design of wallpaper; it is *ornamental design*, which never means anything, and is not the design used by the painter to convey his message with clarity and emphasis. It is natural that this phase of his work should be sought by manufac-

* The Germans, for whom technical lessons assume tremendous importance, have conscientiously studied the principles of Matisse's color and have established schools under the leadership of his pupils, notably a certain Herr Hoffman. Much of German Modernism—excepting of course Surrealist and subjective art—can therefore be traced to this Frenchman.

turers of textiles. He has enjoyed a great vogue among smart women who have found his ingenious decorative talents suited to their taste in upholstery materials, dress goods, etc.

Dufy's significance, however, lies elsewhere than in the technical turn taken. He is above every other Modernist the gay Parisian. Gayety leaps from his canvases, his paint sings. There is no scene so banal that subjected to his brush will fail to yield an amusing and interesting facet. Of late he has made his decorative motifs subservient to a more classical composition (Fig. 33). His pictures are better organized. But this organization is done so easily and spontaneously that only the student is conscious of it. If Lhote (whose work we shall discuss later) is the spokesman of French theorists, Dufy is the principal exponent of French freshness and frivolity.

A painter who studied with the two mentioned above, without allying himself to the group of Wild Beasts, is Rouault. He denies that he was affected by the principles and theories of the group, but his work speaks more loudly for him. The primitive approach, the ill proportions of the early Christians, the heavy rhythmic outlines ally him in technique with Matisse. But Rouault differs from most of the Fauves in that *he has something to say*. His spirit dominates his canvases. In his paintings of repulsive prostitutes and dance-hall types he has something of Van Gogh's fearlessness, but not his objectivity. He is frankly brutal and bitter. He shows himself an idealist, a sort of

204

masochistic hater of humanity and lover of God. His early experience as a designer of stained glass may have affected his pictorial technique, but there is no question of his strong religious feeling in his Biblical pictures.

The picture reproduced, *The Baptism of Christ* (Fig. 34) possesses the same quality that we have seen in primitive Christian art. The figures have the same ludicrous proportions which marked the ascetic cartoons of the catacombs. But there is an added charm. The heavy rhythmic lines and the patterns of light give the canvas a decorative quality similar to that of a stained glass window.

In Braque's work we have the beginnings of a more substantial theory of art than those preached or exploited by the other Fauves. In the still-life reproduced (Fig. 35), we trace easily the influence of Rouault. There is the heavy black rhythm, the same strong patterns of white. In color Braque equals and perhaps surpasses Matisse in the invention of strange harmonies. His picture, too, is not treated as an indeterminate area of little decorative snatches as Dufy's landscapes are, but possesses orthodox composition. There is unity and a center of interest. So that we see in his work all the good qualities of the Fauves. And in addition to these qualities of new rhythm, new color harmonies and good composition, he adds something of the principles of Cezanne and Seurat.

He sees planes. He does not use them as Cezanne did to express form, roundness, volume. But he finds in planes a decorative beauty and detaches them from the object in which they appear. For instance, in the still-life shown here, he paints the pitcher not as it appears in nature, but according to his new theory. He separates a plane of dark in a severe geometric shape so that we see it as a design in itself and also as part of the pitcher. It was in Seurat's work that he saw the possibilities of geometric forms in arbitrary arrangement.

This is the principle which was carried further in the experiments of the Cubists. Braque himself attempted to extract from objects only their planes and lines, and rearrange them into a picture. The result was called Cubism, since the illusion of space and the third dimension was supposedly heightened by this method. It has also been called Purism, although this term has come to have a special significance which we shall explain later. But whether the thing is called "a synthesis of abstraction" or "a cross section" of a group of objects, the whole point of the movement is that the Cubists attempted to do with planes what Matisse attempted to do with color, that is, to separate them from their objects and make a beautiful design of them.

To us Braque is the perfect example of the French modern painter. He is a theorist, an inventor, and above all a Classicist. His painting comes from the head, not from the heart. He accepts the limitations of the art of painting as imposed by the French tradition and within these limitations performs astounding mental acrobatics. He is a laboratory painter. That is to say he paints for the

206

admiration of painters not for that of the people. Compared to such a moralist as Rouault he appears sophisticated, aloof, more concerned with the problems of paint than with those of humanity.

Braque was not alone in this new field of abstract expression or decoration, whichever you will. The versatile Picasso joined him in carrying out the theory of decorative planes. We see in his still-life (Fig. 36) a more rigid pattern than Braque's, a more naïve (or pseudo-naïve) drawing, and a grotesque distortion. (For purposes of design he has made the mandolin handle curve like the trunk of an elephant.) But on the whole there is no great difference between the two pictures.

Here we speak of an innovation of the Cubists, which, no longer indispensable to Cubism, has become almost a tenet of Surrealists. This is the matter of texture. Picasso and his followers in their search for variety of texture concocted compositions of pieces of newspapers, tinfoil, wool, plaster and any other material pleasing to their fancy. When it became apparent that any young girl could manufacture pictures no whit less esthetic by means of a scissors and a pot of paste, the artists perceived the weakness of their method (or were they simply aroused to jealousy?) and abandoned it for a more subtle and difficult one. They simulated textures with paint, which was after all the means of Velasquez. But where Velasquez attained surface by means of accurate values, the Cubists succeeded by differences in technique—the way of putting on the pigment. In one place the paint was stuck on in little lumps; in another it was rubbed in with a chamois; in a third it was striped by the teeth of a comb. Today some Surrealists attain variety in surface by using No. 2 flat inside white in one pattern and glossy white enamel in the corner opposite. But let us return to the Cubists.

In the work of Gleizes, Metzinger, Leger (Fig. 55) and others, the Cubist theory reached its logical end. We see it as a sterile art, the *reductio ad absurdum* of Seurat's and Cezanne's worthy efforts to purify art from reality. It serves today only as advertising art and decoration, no longer novel, but still useful in the applied arts and architecture. While it strove at times to create spatial relation, it seldom attained anything more than pattern.

17

THE NAÏVE AND
"REPULSIVE" PAINTERS

⋙·⋙·⋘·⋘

THE INSPIRATION derived from primitive peoples, first by Gauguin, then by the Fauves, and perhaps best exhibited by Rouault, continued to stimulate a bored society. But it resulted in nothing quite as naïve and childish as was produced by the natural talents of a Parisan who knew nothing about primitive art. This man was Henri Rousseau. His ambition was to paint photographic pictures which would be accepted for exhibition by the Academy. His serious attempts were so ludicrous that they became the rage of smart society.

There was nothing in the man to distinguish him from the class of small tradesman to which he belonged. He loved to paint. But it was only after he was retired from his position in the Department of Customs that he was able to devote himself seriously to his art. His belated ambition to have a picture accepted by the old-fashioned Salon spurred him to laborious effort. Here in America we have seen the paintings done in their spare time by provincial tonsorial artists and the like, and they furnish a few of us amusement. But in a bored Paris eager for novelty Rousseau's careful, minute and artless copying of what was before him elicited the ecstatic praise of critics who were in search of naïveté. He was hailed as a great artist because he expressed naturally what sophisticated painters like Matisse were struggling to achieve—the simplicity of a child.

In spite of his point of view or limitations, his pictures do possess two art qualities. In color they are interesting. In pattern they show great ingenuity. His patterns are in the nature of decorative silhouettes, relieved by little spots or floral designs. He loves the jungle and takes great pains to show as accurately as possible the proper delineation of the flora and fauna. But he does it with the skill of the botanist and the decorator rather than from the point of view of the painter.

In the picture reproduced (Fig. 37) we find a sharp, decorative pattern of silhouettes similar to the design of Breughel. If we turn back to the latter's *Winter* we may see how

210

48. FIGURE STUDY—DERAIN
Courtesy Valentine Gallery

49. THE PORT OF TOULON—FRIESZ

50. FOOTBALL—LHOTE

51. SAILOR'S CONCERT—LHOTE

much more interesting are the decorative silhouettes of the Flemish painter. While Breughel's art is complex, involved, sweeping and rapid in its movement, however popular, *the art of the painter*, Rousseau's is childishly simple, static, *the art of the people*.

The same ingénu temperament is apparent in a painter of Paris scenes who is considered one of the most important of the younger men today. Maurice Utrillo is more interesting as a character than his forerunner. He is a dipsomaniac with infinite patience. Just as Rousseau might have made an excellent botanist, Utrillo might have been a good architect. He has a passion for drawing carefully the outlines of windows and lettering the words on the "affiches." But he is far more of a painter than Rousseau, achieving new combinations and harmonies of color mainly in the use of soft reds and grays or other neutrals. It is said that he derives as much pleasure copying picture post-cards as in working on the scene, and that he achieves his queer, sharp color by working in the light of an oil lamp. No intellectual theories bother him.

There is nothing to say about the picture reproduced (Fig. 38) except that it is amusing in its drawing of the figures in the street and that it lacks the painting qualities, aside from color, which we have looked for in the art of all periods.

Now although the cult of the naïve has had great vogue, it found its adherents, priests, and practitioners mainly in Germany, Russia, and elsewhere in Eastern Europe.

France is too rational a country to be satisfied for long
with an art which is a denial of the mind of man. The
fresh vitality derived from a study of the primitives
restored some life to a painting suffering from sugar in
its watery blood. But the childish concepts of an undevel-
oped man proved to be a false basis for any new art.

A painter who based his own ideals of beauty on those
of the primitives without descending to the banal and the
comical was Modigliani.

It is only since his death in 1920 that the world has
come to value him as one of the most important artists
of the first quarter of the century. His life was quite as
romantic as Gauguin's despite the fact that his short career
as painter was spent in the garrets and cafés of Montmartre. At the age of thirty-five he died of undernourish-
ment and tuberculosis. The horror of his life is translated
into the tender fancies of his pictures. The dreamy visions
born of a wretched existence are made startlingly real by
the sensitive drawing and color of this introverted Italian
Jew.

Let us look at his *Nude*(Fig. 39).It is plainly not the objective approach or attitude that has created it. It is not like the
nudes of Renoir, for instance. Instead it is sentimental,
tender, but without the cheapness that most often accom-
panies sentimental pictures. The pose and the distortion
are reminders of Byzantine Christs. Again there is something in the languorous position of the head that calls to
mind Botticelli. Looking back to the picture of Botticelli's

212

Spring, we see how similar in feeling the two pictures are.

We note the simple beauty of line in the figure. The long, exaggerated line of the face is a continuation of the round line of the shoulder and almost flows into the line of the other shoulder. The line of the hair flows into the curve of the breast. The line of the arm which is partly hidden from view is continued by the shadow of the abdomen. Throughout the lines have a rhythmic grace that is rare. There is none of the harshness which characterizes the work of the Fauves. The color is used, not as decoration, as Matisse uses it, but to express pattern and form as the Florentines used it. The head, the abdomen, the thighs successfully give the illusion of volume. So that we find in the painting enough qualities to establish it as art.

But what interests us most is the *conception,* the unreal charm of the distorted figure. The lady's curious beauty fascinates us, even though we should not care to accompany her to a bathing beach. She is beautiful without conforming to the standards of beauty generally held. The artist has shown us a new aspect of beauty. He has made clear to us his ideal by stressing or exaggerating those characteristics which are present, in more natural proportions, in *many* women. He is advertising no particular model, he is telling us what in woman appears beautiful to him. And so, to impress upon us the beauty of a long, slender face, he has drawn it much longer and much more slender than we are apt to see it in nature. The bulging round thighs seem exceptionally heavy and solid in contrast to the flat

213

breasts and slender body, the ascetic torso of the Byzantines. It is this stress, this distortion which, added to the flowing, rhythmic line and the languid pose, give this nude a place in the art of all time.

In an earlier chapter we said that Renoir was perhaps the world's greatest painter of nudes. It will only lead to confusion, however, to judge an art such as Modigliani's by the standards or precepts of Renoir. It is possible to enjoy both, yet each will find its warmest appreciation in the partisan eyes of realist or idealist. For we have exemplified in their work the two opposite concepts of art: the objective and subjective. Renoir descends from Rubens, Modigliani from El Greco. One dwells on the earth and sings the charms of the flesh, the other plays with the forms of his unattainable paradise. There is nothing wild or orgiastic in Modigliani's hymns to the spirit, but that is because his heritage of gentleness precluded turbulence. The painter Vlaminck writes of him in awestruck prose, calling him a prince among mortals, a man who, whatever his condition, was never lacking in grandeur and in generosity—one who was incapable of a base thought or action. This characterization of the man is congruous with the spirit of his canvases. It also explains why he preferred to die of starvation.

A less sensitive inventor of new beauty is Marcel Gromaire. He is less poet, but more painter. He too shows the influence of the primitives, his figures possessing the form of Giotto and the proportions of early Christian sculp-

214

ture. He reduces his people to a geometric simplicity which recalls Seurat, but endows them with a volume never attained by the Post-Impressionist. Seurat's influence, however, is everywhere apparent—in the manner in which the spots of color are applied, in the rigid architectural masses and simple patterns. But occasionally Gromaire reveals an objectivity similar to Van Gogh's, especially in his paintings of laborers, and a heavy rhythmic line reminiscent of Rouault's.

In the picture here reproduced (Fig. 40) these qualities are easily traced. There is, in the reduction of all forms to their most elementary geometric shape, an approach to Cubism. The planes, volumes, lines are treated abstractly almost in the manner of the Cubists. But it is the new concept of beauty in the figure of the girl rowing that gives Gromaire a greater significance than he would otherwise possess.

New concepts of beauty are not to be confused with repulsiveness. A great artist may show us something beautiful in a face or figure that has previously appeared ugly and repulsive to us. But the artist whose purpose it is to shock us by serving us something he himself finds unredeemingly ugly is motivated by an impulse foreign to art. He is an illustrator or satirist—a commentator on life.

Such is the case of the German, George Grosz, who has had a great influence upon Continental painters. He is preoccupied with matters relating mainly to sex. He seems fascinated by the task of depicting repulsive nudes conceived only in terms of sex. What can be the basic reason

215

for the urge of many European Modernists to dwell upon sexual matters with a bitterness that is too often sly?

A tired, old, disillusioned Continent is taking delight in ridiculing itself. The artist, bitterly regretting the passing of purity, love, the pristine and elemental emotions, is consoling himself by making hideous faces. The urge to paint harlots is perhaps a hysterical protest against the lack of virgins. The charge has been made that painters preoccupied with sex are psychopathic. This we shall consider in the next chapter.

Let us return to Grosz. We print a reproduction of his famous *Hymn to Beauty* (Fig. 41). The scene is a European café. Important-looking gentlemen, probably the trustees of institutions, are sitting around bored and over-fed with diversion. They don't know where to go, they just sit. In the rear, the man with the monocle is impervious to the questioning glance of the questionable lady. In the foreground we have a portrait of a harlot. That is the way they look to the artist, and that is the way they sit in some European cafés.

This commentary on civilized existence is as ironic and as cutting as any that has come from a disillusioned and scornful painter. In its poignant ridicule it offers us the ugly in order to shock us to an ethical readjustment. It is not an unfamiliar concept of a new beauty.

Examined for painting qualities it reveals its artistic deficiencies on another score. The design is haphazard. There *is* pattern, as we can readily see by turning the

216

picture upside down. There are definite areas of different size and shape. But there are too many, and they seem altogether unrelated. There is not the unified, single idea of building up the composition in such a way that we are led slowly and surely to the center of interest. We must be told something and with a tremendous lack of subtlety we are hit in the eye by the chief figure, the nude.

There is no attempt at form, everything is flat.

What, then, is our estimate of this canvas. Plainly it is literature. It is illustration. It is a commentary on life made by means of a picture, but so expressed as to remove our interest from the picture itself to the pitiful situation of these disillusioned idle men and the awful lack of younger, less battered women in the cafés of Europe. Instead of art the picture is a satire done in paint.

It seems that only in France are the traditions of the museum, the qualities in painting, put before every other consideration by artists. The English must tell their stories at all cost; the Germans must sentimentalize and philosophize; the Russians depict their fanciful visions. But in France novelty does not mean new subject matter, but rather new ways of using form, design, rhythm, etc. So that repulsion and ugliness for its own sake is not a French ambition.

The most recent luminary in the firmament of "repulsive" painters is the Russian-Jew, Soutine. His distortion is so generous and uncontrolled as to appear orgiastic (Fig. 42). While his swirling, impetuous technique is derived from

217

Van Gogh, as is much of his technical courage, he has nothing of the Dutchman's genius in seeing only the salient aspects of things. Soutine is not in the least objective. Nor are his horrible looking people the creation of a bitter, hateful onlooker. They are the expression of a neurotic who is saturated with the savage, childish mysticism of his Hebrew heritage. The frenzied rituals and superstitions of his Jewish environment in Vilna have left in him a morbid urge to express his emotional fancies by means of distorted figures. Psychologically his painting springs from a spirit similar to El Greco's. But the great Spanish Greek was more articulate, he had learned the mastery of his craft, and he was sufficiently sensual, in respect to his love for the elements of good painting, to keep his craft on the same high plane as his spirit. Soutine is more poet than painter, and most of all, high priest of the synagogue.

We shall leave for last the group of painters who have built upon the principles of their forerunners, the Fauves and the Post-Impressionists, and have used them for the expression of their own more restrained personalities. This group is exercising the greatest influence in painting to-day. Before investigating their methods, however, let us stop to look at a flickering but significant phase of Modernism. It seems that this is the logical time and place to review briefly the work of the Post-War Expressionists who developed the new art of "psychology in paint."

218

52. HOUSE NEAR THE ROAD–VLAMINCK
Courtesy Balzac Galleries

53. LANDSCAPE–SEGONZAC
Courtesy Valentine Gallery

55. DISKS—LEGER

54. PORTRAIT—KISLING

18

THE EXPRESSIONISTS
AND
PSYCHOPATHIC PAINTERS

⇒⇒⇒⇐⇐

THE WORLD WAR affected painting in several ways in addition to depriving it of a number of its practitioners. If artists reflect their times, the task of post-war painters was clearly cut out for them. With the end of hostilities there came a period of joyous hysteria, a natural reaction to horrors and impending horrors. This period was, generally speaking, one of amorality, called more expressively, "The Age of Jazz"—of noise created out of happy abandon.

In America the spirit of abandon served for the breaking down of moral restrictions and Puritanism. Prohibition itself may have been devised by sedate stay-at-homes to prevent a wilder release of emotions than did actually occur. But in France, which is free of moral restraint, the joyous spirit meant only that war was at an end. Paris went back to the sensible pursuit of gayety that has endeared her to the idlers of the world. She danced and theorized.

Other European nations may have thought her a frivolous jade to have forgotten so soon. But their art students resumed the holy pilgrimage to her cafés and art schools just the same. The tables in front of the Café Dome and the Café Rotonde, for years the havens of foreign artists, flowed over the sidewalk.

Yet for once in the long unbroken stretch of French supremacy in painting, these other countries were making art history while Paris marked time, or rather, learned the fox-trot. It was not that French painters were letting their colors dry up in the tubes; it was that the French sanity, the French reverence for tradition, made them satisfied to repeat their pre-war successes. They painted more than ever and as well as ever, but they seemed completely untouched by the war, emotionally.

The painters of other nations, less rational, more profoundly sensitive, returned to their brushes with all their notions of civilization topsy-turvy. Something terrible had happened to the world and it had left its mark upon them.

220

The meanings of things were now changed. Art no longer meant the trivial pictures in the museums. Beauty was inconsequential, of no importance to a poverty-stricken world.

Painters sat before their easels meditating on the meaning of life in this chaotic universe. They became involved in philosophy, in the magic of numbers, in Hindoo occultism, and any other mental device which could shed some light on the wherefores of existence. These preoccupations they attempted to express with paint. Their aims were diverse, unorganized. Some picked up the threads of Redon's symbolism, others tried to be more naïve than the amusing Rousseau, still others had their meanings in painted riddles. Their quest for a new art, something more vital than the unperturbed objectivity of the French, led them to many novel and curious experiments. Scholars feared for the sanity of these introspective painters. For instance, Professor Oliver Tonks, of Yale University, wrote in the *Arts Magazine* some time in 1924 as follows:

"The modernist artist is ... thoroughly introspective. In a way he is somewhat psycho-analytical, and like most psycho-analytically inclined individuals, he runs the risk of becoming psychopathic. This is borne out by the appearance in modernist literature and painting of works which take an obvious pleasure in dealing with sex problems in a peculiarly raw fashion. This interest in sexual matters is one of the most common manifestations in psychopathic subjects. Not that ... the tendency means that all modernist artists are sex perverts, but there is an

221

unpleasant possibility that too much introspection is not healthy."

Before hastening to share Professor Tonks's alarm we must recall Æsop's fable of the ass in the lion's skin. How much lion we are does not depend upon how much skin we clothe ourselves in. If it is a reaction or vogue to be naïve, childish, preoccupied with sex, algebra, or mystic lore, we are no more psychopathic in following these trends than Miss Pankhurst's ladies were when they wore bloomers. Painters and ladies wished to attract attention to themselves just as much as they wished to express their protests against an unsatisfactory order.

Again we must remember that there is no sharp line of demarcation between the sane and the insane. We all have mental lapses as well as physical. The difference is that we have been educated to admit our physical disabilities while disregarding or denying our mental ones. There are millions of drugstores which pander to our little attacks of cold and indigestion, but it is only when we are completely wrecked mentally that we receive attention. So that the difference between the sane and the insane may be determined only by the frequency and intensity of the mental lapse.

Even this presents difficulties. Was Van Gogh sane or insane? His writings are wise, calm, sensitive, observant. His actions are those of a madman. His paintings best reveal his states of mind. At times he is the observer such

222

as Courbet was, dispassionate and objective. At other times he is wild, strenuous, excited. *But in no respect is this excited painting comparable to the painting of asylum inmates.* His work is distinguished by its color, color relations, movement, organization. The work of inmates is marked by a conscious attempt to attain precise brushwork or technique, while remaining completely impervious to the qualities of painting which give pleasure to the sane painter.

The insane inmate's picture is often similar in subject matter to those reproduced in this chapter. Religion and occultism are second in choice only to sex eroticism. But the insane painter in nearly every instance marks his picture with interpretative inscriptions. And as Dr. Prinz-horn shows in his *Bilderei der Gefangenen,* the underlying urge back of the feeble-minded painter is that of expressing some moral or technical concept or some palliative to conscience. The most significant difference, however, is that already stated: The sane painter *organizes* his picture; he will consider *qualities* above subject. The insane painter, like the child, wishes only to tell his story in an elaborate system of hieroglyphics.

Where there are no qualities apparent in the work of the sane painter we are inclined to the opinion that he is consciously *imitating* the insane painter, like the ass in the lion's skin, in an effort to appear occult. We like to play at being bad men, or cave-men, so there is no reason why we shouldn't like to pretend that we are insane

223

occasionally, especially if we have terribly sound minds. The really insane person does not wish to be unintelligible as his imitator does. Because his product is decipherable to himself he assumes that it is clear to all. An amusing illustration of this appeared recently in a German humorous paper.

A visitor to an asylum saw a patient using a dry brush on a piece of canvas.

"What does that represent?"

"The Flight of the Children of Israel from Egypt."

"Where are the children of Israel?"

"They have passed over the Red Sea."

"Where is the Red Sea?"

"Rolled back."

"Where are the Egyptians?"

"They are expected every minute."

Keeping the above differences in mind let us look at the work of the German and Russian Expressionists. Three influences will be apparent in them. First, the cultivation of the primitive and the naïve which was begun by Gaugin and carried to amusing absurdity in the work of Rousseau; second, the Cubist and Purist love of lines, colors, and forms for their own sake, which we have seen exemplified in the work of Braque and Picasso; third, and perhaps most important, the symbolism of Redon.

From art as tenderly poetic and as fanciful as the nude of Modigliani which we left in the last chapter, it is an easy and natural step to the visions of Chagall. However

224

outwardly different is *The Anniversary* (Fig. 43), the same tender sentimentalism pervades it; and as in the nude it exists without any hint of heavy banality, without any bid for the sympathy of the spectator. The conception is refined, poetic. We see a husband kissing his wife. Such is his love for her that, at the moment of their kissing, he is not conscious of being rooted to the ground. His soul soars to Heaven. To let you know it, the painter depicts the whole man soaring to Heaven. This is expressionism, the subjective painting of a man's feelings. Its principles are those of Redon, its language more articulate.

The picture is accomplished with a fine understanding of the resources of the painter. The earthly details of the room, the purse, the kitchen utensils, serve to accentuate the *unearthly* joy of the man in greeting his wife. (We should not be completely shocked at the oddity of the conception since we are familiar with Perugino's angels who float in the corners of all his canvases. And in El Greco's *Burial of Count Orgaz* half of the picture is earthly realism and half pure fancy.) The charm of contrast appears again in the use of line. The line of the woman's back is a fluid, rapid, decorative one, certainly as beautiful as Hogarth's famous *Line of Beauty*. The man's legs are drawn arbitrarily, not according to anatomy, but for the sake of the line. The rapid, flowing lines in the figures make us feel the emotion of the two, in contrast to the rigid lines of the table, the windows, the floor.

None of the feebly suggested forms is convincing. But

225

the presence of solid, sculpturesque form would destroy the fancy. This new art of the mind could never be achieved by adhering to the old requirements dictated by the laws of physics. To paint a rock so that we feel its weight requires a different approach than the problem of painting a nervous sensation. Whether the painting of a nervous sensation in terms of fancy is art or not is a question open to discussion. Certainly the picture we are studying holds our interest and gives us a new view of an old emotion.

We must be partial to this Russian painter Chagall, and reproduce another of his pictures, since it is as good an example of *mental processes* as we can find. It is called *I and the Village* (Fig. 44). In the lower center of the canvas is a circle which links the man with the cow. The man looks at the cow smilingly and offers her a delicacy. The cow looks back at him as if to say, "Oh I appreciate your attentions, but you can't fool me. You want my milk." Painted on the cow's cheek (or whatever you would call a cow's cheek) is a picture of what the animal is thinking. In the background is a tired harvester being urged on to the delights of home by an angel standing on her head. If we may be permitted a pun, the angel is at her wit's end to entertain him. The face in the church fills a whole storey. It is meant to show us that every action of the villagers is perceived.

If this picture were merely a puzzle such as children delight to turn upside down to find the face of the admiral, it could be no funnier. But for some reason it is also a very serious picture. We subscribe to its truthfulness. We look

226

at the picture a long time, studying its queer forms and rhythms. The question is: Does the literary quality of the thing, the fact that it starts us off on a spree of speculation about the dumbness of farm life—does this literary quality overweigh our interest in the forms and rhythms?

The German painter Heinrich Campendonck was another leader in this new school of painting. He exerted his influence not only upon his colleagues but upon painters throughout Europe, and in one notable case, upon an American, Carl Knaths. Campendonck's principles differed little from Chagall's, but the temperaments and equipment of the two were totally unlike. Chagall seems always careful of his pattern, always occupied with decorative forms and lines. Campendonck achieves a kind of harmony in his canvases by his distribution of his color in the manner of Matisse. He is a master in balancing his color and keeping it moving, "circulating" it. His drawing and his forms are the most naïve possible, making Rousseau appear, by comparison, artful and sophisticated. Let us look at his picture called *Penzberg* (Fig. 45).

The village is thrown into a state of excitement by the approach of the railroad engine. The cow is so frightened by the noise and the smoke that she behaves as if her head were cut off. The artist shows us the head severed from the body. Other cows are fleeing, terrified, from the stable. Only their heads full of fear exist; the rest of their bodies don't matter. Two women are engaged in conversation. "It's twelve minutes late," the first is probably saying.

227

"Do you think the engineer will stop at our city for a drink?" asks the other. The engine labors up the hill, puffing smoke and cinders, which are represented by black stars.

Certainly the artist conveys to us the importance of the occasion. And in spite of all its naïve illustrative detail, the picture is not illustration. However literary the theme, we are kept *in the picture* and not interested primarily in the storey. The design or composition of the picture is accomplished not only by the excellent distribution of color, but also by means of the diagonal rhythms. Everywhere the lines follow each other. The painting possesses too much art to be classified as a mere cartoon.

A compatriot of Campendonck and a fellow in arms is Paul Klee. With Kandinsky he carried the new psychological art to its most absurd conclusion. He strives so strenuously to be more naïve than a new-born babe, that we exhaust his offerings very quickly. If we dwell at all upon them, it is not to examine the things *in* the canvas but the idea *behind* it. What does it mean? Why does he do it? Evidently there is more hidden meaning in this picture *A Feat of Magic* (Fig. 46) than in a lodge emblem. But it is only for those who are Honorary Fellows and Past Masters of the Rosicrucians to fathom the secret of the scattered letters, the moon, and the botanical display. Since the picture is devoid of any of the qualities present in the others, and since it gives us no new aspect of life, we can

228

only conclude that it is a system of hieroglyphics to which we do not possess the key.

An Italian, Giorgio de Chirico, is considered by some critics the most important of the newer painters. He differs from the others whose work we have reproduced in that he is rigidly classical, not only in his architectural groups and forms, but in his adherence to and mastery of pattern, space, and form. His form is as effective as Giotto's; his color, the most unusual combinations and harmonies of all the Modernists, excepting perhaps Braque.

He does not paint visions and fancies in the manner of Chagall. Nor does he express the thoughts and feelings of the characters in his canvas in the manner of Campendonck. Neither is he naïve. He resembles in his preoccupation with the occult and the metaphysical, Paul Klee. But unlike the German he paints his symbolism with the most serious attention to the traditional qualities of painting, as if he were commissioned to execute his weird philosophies for the Sistine Chapel. He is not modern at all in the sense that the others are. His careful drawing and attention to the laws of composition and perspective are really pre-Renaissance. It is his color and his subject matter that are modern.

The picture which we reproduce is called the *Diviner,* or *Mindreader* (Fig. 47). It is very original in its pattern, full of variety. The space is remarkably well organized. The basilica in the rear and the manikin in the foreground are painted with an understanding of form that is rarely

229

seen. Merely as a composition the picture is art, not only because of its good pattern (that is not enough), but also because it gives us, with intense reality, the feeling of the proper space (spatial relation) between the manikin, the easel, and the building.

What the picture means to say we leave to be determined. A friend in the engineering profession could make nothing of the problem on the blackboard. He insisted that the answer lay elsewhere in the picture, in the phallic symbol of the shadow on the floor. If this is so then here is one of the pictures Professor Tonks was thinking of when he wrote his article on the dangerous trend of Modernism.

19

THE ECLECTICS

⇶⇶⇷⇷

THE PAINTERS grouped in this chapter have been termed by some critics The Eclectics. This is an excellent term, since it conveys at once the intentions of the artists to select all the good points of all the schools coming before them. If they succeeded only in rehashing and combining various styles and personalities, however, their work would achieve no more dignity and worth than that of the "artists" who copy the *Mona Lisa* in the Louvre. They use the *principles*, the personality is their own.

Derain is one of the best known painters of this group. It is difficult to select a picture for reproduction which will embody all his aims and preoccupations. Like the even more celebrated Picasso,* he has worked in many styles and is catalogued according to many periods. First a member of the Fauves, he made use of the heavy black *Fauvian* line to achieve rhythm and design. Then came his most colorful period, in which he put to great use the lessons of Cezanne. Using the same color and the same technique as the "Old Man of Aix," he added to them a severe geometric sense dating back to Seurat.

This theory of complementary planes of vivid color and rigid forms he seems now to have definitely abandoned. He has emerged a "Neo-Old Master," painting in soft red browns and giving to his figure studies and heads a Rembrandtesque quality (Fig. 48). The flesh which he paints does not scintillate; it is of a unified sepia warmth, the passages (or modeling) subtle, and the form held together by a broken, sensitive line recalling Rembrandt's drawings.

* Picasso is not properly an eclectic. He belongs to almost all schools, not as a follower but as a leader. Of all modern innovators he is perhaps the most fertile. The scope of this book does not permit an exposition of his many styles and ideas and periods, all of them extremely interesting but for the most part better exemplified in the single track preoccupations of more simple painters. His recent or "Neo-Classical" period is perhaps his fullest attainment. Here he transposes Greek figures into modern forms. He will paint a Juno in a flat fiery pink and in much ampler form than the Greek ideal. Conservative critics fail to see the connection between these inflated Greek goddesses and modernist principles. We may recall that every revival of Classicism, however much it aims at eternity, bears markedly the stamp of its time and place. The British Pre-Raphaelites were more 1870 British than 1500 Florentine. Similarly classical Greek ideals are translated by Picasso into the idiom of modern painting.

Derain's later landscapes come from the same point of view and from the same palette as his figure studies. Low in tone they are dignified. Brown and deep green seem to exclude all other colors, like many old Dutch scenes. They differ, however, in their bold design and rhythm, in their swelling form and unrealistic organization. They retain the quality of the museum picture while belonging to present-day expression.

Othon Friesz is another member of the Fauves but one who almost from the beginning of his career struck his distinctly personal style. He has combined the rhythmic line of Matisse with the planes of color and spatial relation of Cezanne. He is one of the few Cezannists who has not used the master's theories in a superficial way. He has not *prettified* Cezanne, as most English and American Cezannists feel compelled to do. His paintings are honest in point of view and are not a popular art, his sense of rhythm endowing them with classical composition and movement.

In his *Port of Toulon* (Fig. 49), we see the use of heavy black lines characteristic of the Fauves. The drawing, however, is not distorted. The principal beauty of the canvas is its movement, the design of line, or rhythms, carrying us around and around the harbor. The bustle of the port is transmitted to us. The point of view is impressionistic. There is little intellectual theory; only a rapid statement of nature, but extremely well ordered and honestly presented.

André Lhote is the intellectual painter of theories and

233

traditions. His relation to the group is similar to the relation Seurat bore to the Post-Impressionists. Both painters are linked by their bent for rigid geometrical forms. But the Modernist has added to the theories of his predecessor. Where Seurat was content to achieve geometrical pattern, Lhote has attempted action.

The problem of securing action or movement by rigid, mechanical patterns seems at first glance unlikely of solution. Botticelli demonstrated the efficacy of rhythmic line in securing movement, but graceful line naturally lends itself to the suggestion of flight, the soaring bird, the leaping animal, the flowing gown. Raphael's patterns linking one figure to another by areas of similar color also achieve an impression of activity, but they are pliable, almost liquid in contour. Lhote fused one color pattern into another but he counted mainly upon rhythm to perform its ancient services in a modern cause; with what success we may see in the picture, *Football* (Fig. 50).

We are made to feel the play and not the individual figures. The realistic painters of battle scenes, whose works stock our museums, achieved only portraits of individuals in arrested action, which is after all static. In this experiment of Lhote's, on the other hand, the individual is only part of the play and does not exist by himself. Yet the picture does not hold us for long. A flatness which amounts almost to emptiness discourages our curiosity. The figures, lacking form, cannot keep our interest.

Apparently the artist himself felt the deficiencies of his
234

theory. He eventually abandoned this use of flat patterns in action and has gone to the other extreme in securing form. He now employs cubist principles to a limited extent. The outlines of his forms are stylized and conventional but he does not remove parts of things from the whole; the natural order remains undisturbed. He does not use lines and forms abstractly, he only simplifies, interprets, or "purifies" them. Instead of drawing an arm, for instance, in the usual, literal way, to show the muscular formation, the Purist will reduce the contour to precise round and straight lines.

We reproduce Lhote's *Concert* (Fig. 51) as an example of Purism. The presence of traditional qualities is at once apparent. In the painting of the sailor playing the concertina, the form bulges. Though in no way resembling them, it is yet reminiscent of the figures of Michelangelo. The planes and volumes are sculptural. Spatial relation too is skillfully achieved. And in addition, there is the most inventive design or pattern. Where the picture fails to maintain its distinction is in its lack of vitality or freshness. To us it smacks too much of the mathematical problem correctly worked out. It is too schematic. A certain *spirit* is lacking.

In direct contrast to Lhote is Vlaminck. His pictures have the hasty, emotional quality of a painting by Van Gogh, without at all resembling it in technique. They are essentially impressionistic, like the pictures of Friesz. In color, however, they are unlike anything of the Impressionists or Post-Impressionists. Critics point to Vlaminck's

235

descent from Flemish stock to explain the characteristics of his work which are foreign to Paris. His chiaroscuro, or strong values of light and shade, is traced back to Rembrandt. But this romantic quality is present in the work of all the dramatist-painters, notably Leonardo and El Greco. However, the critics are not to be gainsaid. Certainly the blue which dominates many of his canvases is Antwerp blue.

While not concerned with the theories current among French Modernists, Vlaminck is modern nevertheless by virtue of his efforts to simplify almost to flat areas of color whatever is before him. What is even more important is his success in achieving spatial relations. He profits somewhat from the lessons of Cezanne. While his color is entirely different, making no use of the principle of warm and cool planes, his brush builds the surface into planes, and his darks and lights set each other off in much the same way as Cezanne's contrasting color does. What Vlaminck does not possess is Cezanne's conscientious thoroughness. He achieves his effects in a clever, facile way, so that his pictures have the rapid brilliant charm, as well as the limitations, of a sketch (Fig. 52). Vitality is their principal possession. You have only to turn from a National Academy exhibition of sickly sweet, false and anæmic landscapes to one of Vlaminck's pictures, to realize how far above mere technical accomplishment an artist's honest and personal way of seeing things can be.

The Polish-Jewish painter Kisling is not quite as ob-

236

jective as Vlaminck. He pretends to be not at all concerned with theories, but they have crept into his portraits in spite of himself. His rhythm is almost as well thought out as Modigliani's. His understanding of form is deserving of every painter's respect. His warm glowing color, while not as inventive, is as personal as is that of Matisse. He wishes to be objective and scientific, but a pronounced sentimentality invades his canvases, giving to his urchins and little working-girls much of his own pitying reaction to their poor or meaningless lives. He is as tender as Vlaminck is romantic; but both have sufficient command of their medium to escape the stigma of the term "literary."

There are in America more than a few painters who can paint a head quite as well as the one of Kisling's here reproduced (Fig. 54). But few would dare to paint a hand and arm in such simple geometric shapes as this hand and arm possess. Nor could fashionable painters understand the necessity for the design of line which does not enhance the beauty of the girl. In painting the shawl they would work furiously to catch its texture correctly, but how many would think of making *the line* important? Here the wavy line repeats the similar line made by the face and neck. It carries the eye directly to the face. Its importance is due to the fact that all the other lines are either severely curved or severely straight, without variations. It is the picture which is important to Kisling, not the girl.*

* Some revision of these estimates is necessitated by the painters' recent performances. While wishing to retract nothing we must add the fact that

An intelligent painter who is not concerned with intellectual theories is Segonzac. He wishes only to put down what is before him. Confronted with nature he is calm and simple, neither emotional nor distressed. Rembrandt seems to have influenced him more than has any contemporary. In his still-life studies there are the rich browns of the Flemish and Dutch School, the same point of view combined with a freedom in technique almost as great as Vlaminck's. But although he brings up-to-date the northern attention to somber still-life studies, he seems at his best in his simple paintings of the outdoors. Here he shows his love for thick, juicy gray paint, as well as his love of trees and quiet streams. In a world of sophistication and isms, his pictures have a sanity and freshness which delight us. His painting is neither sentimental nor romantic. He himself would term it realism. It is by no means the same realism that pervades the finicky photographic pictures of the realists of 1850. This we can see in the landscape reproduced (Fig. 53).

men of Vlaminck's stature seem to have succumbed to the universal demand for factory production. Every little boutique of a gallery on the left bank of Paris, every art-bookshop possesses in common with the important dealers one or more Vlamincks. It is hardly necessary to say that they are for the most part too hastily produced and minus inspiration. They have the character of autographs and much the same significance. Painters now speak of Vlaminck's "earlier stuff."

Even worse is true of Kisling. Just as prolific as his confrère, he has definitely bowed down to success. His wistful little children have grown into drooping, pleading, sad-eyed Mimis. Sickly prettiness seems the end desired; to it is sacrificed the subtle full form and delicacy of line which marked the painter's earlier periods.

There is in it a rhythm which owes a great deal to the Fauves. Yet its rustic feeling removes it from the ateliers of Paris. The artist is close to nature. And that he loves as well the actual medium with which he works is shown by the way the appetizing pigment is piled on.

There is no pretension here, as there is not elsewhere in this book, to include the names of all deserving painters. It suffices us to mention only the representatives of certain forms of the art. Today in Paris new painters are coming to the fore who possess as much ability as those mentioned here without in any way revealing new departures. It is true that the Surrealists remain the most novel of all the innovators, displaying such astounding ingenuity and enterprise as to attract still, in this day of blasé indifference, the ire of critics. They have learned too the advisibility of cooperative marketing and organization so that their exhibitions instead of being the puny individualistic "one-man" shows which nobody visits, are a whole barracks-full of astounding brain children—glass eyes stuck on painted faces, drawings done in piano wire and other amusing and ingenious divertisements which give the exhibition the allure of the circus. Nevertheless much fine art is sprinkled about in this Surrealist bombardment of the placid bourgeois.

Coming back to the Eclectics, who it goes without saying, see utter dissolution in Surrealism, we might mention the names of a few of the younger painters who merit a place in the company of those already introduced. Per Krogh

239

and Willy Eisenschitz are two foreign artists who are paying their debt to Paris by infusing its art with a vitality sorely needed in this, it seems to us, twilight of a glorious tradition.

20

CONCLUSION

꧁꧁꧂꧂

NEW TENDENCIES in painting, with the exception of
the experiments of the Post-War Expressionists, have been
in the past century the result of French thought and ingenuity. If the painting of other nations, notably our own,
has not been touched upon in the foregoing chapters it is
not because we wish to sniff at the art of the rest of the
world, but because we are primarily concerned with the
evolution of painting, its trends and innovations.

France can lay no claim to exclusive possession of talent.

There is nothing inherent in the Frenchman to make him automatically a man of genius. What France possesses for the service of art is Paris. Paris is a city lacking in homogeneity. It is a collection of pigeonholes in which every sort of pigeon may come to roost. For this reason the artists of all nations, feeling the subtle hostility of their own environment, come to Paris. And because Paris has a tradition and Frenchmen who can intellectualize the most logical abstractions and lay them down like railroad tracks for foreign locomotives to ride on, Paris takes all the credit. Picasso, Modigliani, Chagall, for example, are called French painters, although Spain, Italy and the Jewish race may glory each in its own son. So that it is perhaps more accurate to say that many European peoples have contributed vitality to Modern art while following French precepts.

The reader may have remarked throughout a certain stress upon the *spiritual* import of pictures. It may seem incongruous with the insistence of the earlier chapters that he judge pictures in the light of knowledge and analysis. To this apparent contradiction the reply is that we may look at an oyster for years but only when we know how to open it may we find the occasional pearl. Only by understanding the painting will the painter's spirit be revealed to us. Besides this practical reason, we confess ourselves partial to subjective painting, as opposed to objective, although it is often difficult to draw the line between them. In the tiring materialism of our world the expression of

242

personal experience or feeling is the last refuge of individual being. It is the heroic challenge of one man's organized sensations flung to meaningless organization of men.

Here, in conclusion, we may summarize our concept of the art of painting. Its function is not to recall a place, thing or experience, but to extend the range of our feelings as learning extends the range of our minds. To give an example: The painter-artist looks at the same scene we have glanced at a thousand times. He paints it when it awakens some response in him. He shows us his picture. The picture so conveys his feeling to us that we are enabled to experience a fresh delight in viewing the scene as if it had never before existed. Thus he extends the range of our feelings. Again, the artist turns away from nature. He paints a dream world, organizes it into a small canvas, and peoples it with brain children. By making us feel upon looking at his picture that we are actually in this strange world of his fancy, he certainly widens our experience, or calls into being new emotions—extends the range of our feelings.

Thus is living given an added dimension and significance. Modernism more than any school of painting since El Greco has approached this concept of the function of art.

THE END